Poetry, Politics
And Dorothy Gone Horribly Astray

CRITICISM

Kevin Higgins

Belfast
LAPWING

First Published by Lapwing Publications
c/o 1, Ballysillan Drive
Belfast BT14 8HQ

British Library Cataloguing in Publication Data.
A catalogue record for this book is available from
the British Library.

ACKNOWLEDGEMENTS

Thanks to the editors of the following publications in which
some of these reviews and essays were previously published:
Nthposition.com, Red Banner, Books in Canada,
The Journal (UK), The Galway Advertiser,
Arts West.

Set in Aldine 721 BT
by
Winepress Services

ISBN 1-905425-40-6

CONTENTS

Poetry, Politics
And Dorothy Gone Horribly Astray

CRITICISM

POETRY, POLITICS AND DOROTHY GONE HORRIBLY ASTRAY

Almost every poet I know is prone to exaggerate the influence poetry can exert on world events. Maybe it's the cold reality of poetry's marginal position in society which leads many of us, particularly at a time of crisis like this, to talk in loud excited voices about how poetry can supposedly make politicians sit up and listen or even 'change the world'. This benign egocentricity is perhaps a necessary indulgence to save us from vanishing entirely into our garrets, or academia, convinced of the total irrelevance of what we do. If we don't at least convince ourselves that poetry can matter, then how on earth can we expect to convince anyone else?

The truth is poetry can sometimes play a role in actually changing people's minds, by convincing the reader (or listener) emotionally of an idea to which he or she may be intellectually opposed. If a poem can win the ideologically hostile reader's heart, then his or her head will surely follow. Such a heightened experience of poetry can lead to a transformed world view for the reader. So, yes, the influence of poetry can be profound.

However, the power of poetry is more elusive, less tangible than that exerted by politicians and generals. Yes, poems such as Wilfred Owen's *Dulce Et Decorum Est* and W.H. Auden's *September 1 1939* continue to exert power over readers all these decades later. But in his lifetime Wilfred Owen's poetry failed to shorten by a day the war that, in its last week, claimed his life. And for all its warnings, the glittering genius of Auden could do nothing to stall humanity's mad march to Auschwitz and Hiroshima. That's just not how it works. And despite our sometimes inflated sense of ourselves, deep down most of us know that, during his famous afternoon lie-downs, George W. Bush probably doesn't lose a moment's shut-eye worrying about people like us. One doesn't get to be President of the United States, or President of anywhere, by caring what poets think.

Generally speaking, if the government does something of which we disapprove - such as sending back illegal immigrants, giving the police more powers, or cutting spending on the Arts - it is probably a measure their heartland constituency, in Kansas or the Home Counties, quietly approves of. The disaster that lurks around George W. Bush's bed these days - and must soon shake even him awake - is precisely the way opposition to his colonial adventure in Iraq has now worked its way into the heartland. (In Tony Blair's case the opposition to the war has long-since captured the heartland; for him the argument is lost.)

In Galway on the West coast of Ireland, where I live, I have listened to everyone from the taxi-driver to the postman to the old woman in the launderette spit poison against George W. Bush. I spent my teenage years foaming at the mouth every time President Reagan appeared on television, while my American relatives loudly supported him. Last Sunday I had a telephone conversation with my uncle John, a retired construction foreman in Chicago, and he was angrier about Bush than the teenage me ever was about Reagan. The other week I spoke to my partner Susan's stepmother in Philadelphia; a woman, who has been very good to us over these last few years, but who also happens to be a gun-owning, pro-death penalty registered Republican. She told me that in November, because of the war, she would be voting for "anyone but Bush". And, no, she wasn't just playing to the gallery of the pinko son-in-law-to-be. When it comes to politics this woman is more likely to invite you to an NRA convention, than she is to spare your feelings in such a soggy, sentimental way.

Paradoxically, the fact that opposition to the Iraq adventure is now so widespread has made writing poetry about it very difficult; poetry and consensus make bad bedfellows. At least that's been my experience. In the aftermath of 9/11 I found it easy enough to write poems about the attack on the Twin Towers, the War in Afghanistan etc. Lately I have found it impossible to address the Iraq issue in poetry. Back then one was taking a risk by saying anything about the War On Terror; and risk makes for good poetry. Now, all one is doing when one writes a straightforward anti-war poem is agreeing with the old woman in the launderette, and pretty much everyone else on the planet. When the whole world is saying the same thing the words get used up and jaded, and we start to sound like newscasters rather than poets.

Poets are often guilty of indulging in hyperbole when talking about political issues, but it is difficult to overstate the extent of the disaster now facing the Coalition in Iraq. In early 2003 the Bush/Blair arguments for war were: (1) Saddam Hussein had weapons of mass-destruction which he would not hesitate to use against the West, Israel and his own people; (2) Saddam Hussein was a bloodthirsty despot who ruled by murder and torture; and (3) under Saddam Hussein, Iraq had become an operational base for al-Qaeda.

We now know that there were no weapons of mass-destruction. This is something we tend to shrug off a little too easily. Just because we believed all along that Bush and Blair were lying about the existence of WMDs in Iraq does nothing to lessen the significance of the fact that every thinking person in both the US and Britain now knows for sure that their respective governments looked them in the eye in late 2002/early 2003 and told barefaced lies about such an important issue. In March 2003 most people in Britain believed Tony Blair was wrong about Iraq, but they certainly did not believe he was a ruthless liar. Now that truth is unavoidable. If this wasn't bad enough, the Blair government's attempts to coerce the BBC into covering the issue up is blamed by a large proportion of the British public for the suicide in Oxfordshire last summer of a softly-spoken Government scientist, Dr David Kelly. There will be no coming back from that for Tony.

Like a worn-out animal, he'll stumble on a while longer, but must surely soon find a quiet place to politically die. Perhaps after the European elections. Perhaps a little later.

No-one has ever argued that Saddam Hussein was anything but a bloodthirsty tyrant; I'm sure that's how he'd describe himself in the unlikely event of being asked for a résumé by a prospective employer. However, since the release of the photographs from Abu Ghraib prison, the problem for the US is it now seems that the difference between Saddam's regime and their occupying forces is less about fundamentals than it is about degree. Okay, so (as far as we know) the US army don't actually dissolve their opponents in acid-baths, as Saddam famously did. But they do force prisoners to strip, tie what looks like a green plastic bag over each prisoner's head, and then pile naked prisoners on top of each other like carcasses in an abattoir. Only these are human beings. And then they take photographs. The last people crazy enough to go out of their way to create such damning evidence of their own war crimes were the Khmer Rouge.

For me, the most bizarre photograph is one which shows Specialist Charles A. Graner of the US Army wearing a particularly silly smile and a pair of turquoise gloves, his arms folded as he gives the camera the thumbs up. In front of him stands Specialist Sabrina Harman. She is bending over, and smiling, looking for all the world like Dorothy from the Wizard of Oz gone horribly astray. Immediately in front of her are a pile of naked, hooded Iraqi prisoners.

At this point, I should say that if offered a choice between being dissolved in sulphuric acid and being stripped naked and forced to lie in a pile of similarly naked prisoners, I think I'd generally choose the latter. Life is almost always better than death. But it's not much of a choice. And it certainly has nothing at all to do with freedom or democracy. As British Conservative MP Boris Johnson has said: before these photographs, the Coalition could at least claim that, whatever else, political prisoners were no longer being tortured in Iraqi jails. Now that too has been lost. And like Tony Blair's integrity, it won't be coming back. From now on we can expect many more such photographs. Some will no doubt be hoaxes. But enough will turn out to be true.

The centre of Galway is now covered in posters for a rally to protest against George W. Bush's visit to Ireland on Saturday June 26th. The posters use a photograph of Private Lynndie England holding a dog-leash at the end of which is a naked Iraqi prisoner, and the simple but superbly effective slogan "This Torturer Used Shannon Airport". The Irish Government's decision to allow US Military aircraft to refuel at Shannon has been a particular bone of contention here. I spotted at least three posters from which Lynndie England's face had been burned away with a cigarette.

And from an apartment complex in Dominick Street, an American flag now hangs upside-down. It is one of the Bush administration's outstanding achievements, that they have managed to turn the overwhelming pro-American sympathy that was the Irish reaction to the attack on the Twin Towers into this sort of bitter hostility. But their achievements don't end there.

The objective of the 'War On Terror' was supposed to be the defeat of al-Qaeda. In March 2003 the network was non-existent in Iraq. However, a few weeks ago the leader of their newly founded Iraqi section, Abu al-Zarqawi, beheaded Nick Berg, a 26 year-old businessman from Westchester, Pennsylvania, and broadcast the execution on the Internet. Berg is heard to say "My name is Nick Berg, my father's name is Michael, my mother's name is Suzanne. I have a brother and a sister. David and Sarah. I live in Philadelphia." Then the knife is ruthlessly applied. Berg's headless body was found on the outskirts of Baghdad. Nick Berg's father Michael was quoted as saying "Nicholas Berg died for the sins of George Bush and Donald Rumsfeld. The al-Qaeda people are probably just as bad as they are - but this administration did this." The whole situation is starting to look like a trap of al-Qaeda's making, into which America sleepwalked in the aftermath of 9/11. Wherever Osama Bin Laden is tonight, he must be laughing horribly into his beard.

There'll be no easy solutions here. Even if Kerry wins in November, Iraq will continue to crack into at least three pieces. And as long as American troops remain - and don't kid yourself, John Kerry certainly won't withdraw them - the more fundamentalist leaders will continue to gain support. Just as al-Qaeda is not a liberation movement with whom the European or American left could ever make common cause, the Shia cleric Muktadr Al-Sadr is no Ho Chi Minh or Che Guevara. What is opening up now in Iraq is a catastrophe.

And the world, from New York to Madrid to Bali, is wracked by a conflict between a Texan buffoon, who by his own admission can't be bothered to read the newspapers or listen to the television news, and a batty Saudi aristocrat out restore the seventh- century Islamic Caliphate, which at its zenith stretched from the Persian Gulf to Spain. Not a good situation. As activists and writers, the best we can do for now is avoid parroting pretend solutions - the last thing the world needs to hear is more untruths, even well-meaning ones - and bear witness as honestly and as well as we possibly can, be it in poetry or be it in prose.

April, 2004

BORGES, BALZAC & THE GHOST OF CHRISTMAS YET TO COME
A review of *Unacknowledged Legislation: Writers In The Public Sphere* by Christopher Hitchens, Verso 17.00 (hardback)

To say that the relationship between literary criticism and Marxist politics has been fraught with difficulties is something of an understatement. More often than not the nuanced, dialectical approach used by the likes of Marx and Trotsky to unravel the world of literature in all its many sided complexity has been (and for the most part still is) elbowed aside in favour of a crude reductionism which has its origins in the Stalinist crackdown on literature and art in the late 1920s. Even today, those who review books (or films) for left-wing publications tend to operate on the basis that if a book is 'objectively speaking' on the right side of the class struggle then this, in and of itself, must mean that the book in question is a 'good book' deserving a positive review. And the reverse is also held to be true: T. S. Eliot's poetry couldn't possibly be a patch on, say, Jimmy McGovern's *Dockers* because, after all, T.S.Eliot was a reactionary. In the minds of some, any comrade who takes a few hours out from the class struggle to read *The Wasteland* or *The Love Song of J. Alfred Prufrock* is probably in serious danger of ending up on the Fine Gael front-bench or as Primate of the Church of Ireland or some such grotesque bourgeois deviation.

Roddy Doyle is judged to be more 'politically relevant' than, say, John Updike or Julian Barnes, because he writes about 'ordinary working class people', whereas they for the most part don't. And indeed perhaps he is more relevant, at least in the sense that his subject matter means that socialists will probably have more to say about him than they will about most contemporary novelists. However, taken too far, this sort of approach to literature and art could, at least in theory, reduce us to the absurdity of saying that Brendan Grace is somehow a better comedian than Woody Allen merely because his subject matter is more 'working-class'; or, perhaps a little more plausibly, that Rage Against The Machine are definitely better than Elgar was, because they sing 'fuck the police', whereas he did nothing of the sort. Marx may have thought that, in literary terms, one reactionary Balzac, writing as he did predominantly about the French middle and upper classes, was preferable to a hundred socialist Zolas, writing about 'the workers', but such dialectical niceties tend unfortunately to be lost on most of his followers.

In this context, Christopher Hitchens' *Unacknowledged Legislation: Writers In The Public Sphere* is required reading for anyone even remotely interested in the relationship between literature and politics. And how ironic it is that this example of a dialectical (one might say almost Marxist) approach to literature should be provided by Hitchens: a 'left' liberal *Vanity Fair* columnist, who since September 11th has apparently lost the run of himself and become (along with silly old Paul McCartney) just another raving imperialist warmonger.

It is, as Margaret Thatcher once famously remarked, a funny old world indeed.

The book is a collection of thirty five reviews and essays, which originally appeared in publications such as The New York Review of Books, The New Left Review & The Times Literary Supplement. In the foreword Hitchens tells us about the influence Wilfred Owen's devastatingly powerful anti-war poem *Dulce Ft Decorum Est* had on him as a young man:

"I shall never be able to forget the way in which these verses utterly turned over all the furniture in my mind; inverting every conception of order and patriotism and tradition on which I had been brought up. I hadn't yet encountered, or even heard of the novels of Barbusse and Remarque, or the paintings of Otto Dix, or the great essays and polemics of the Zimmerwald and Kienthal conferences; the appeals to civilisation written by Rosa Luxembourg in her Junius incarnation. (Revisionism has succeeded, in overturning many of the icons of Western Marxism; this tide however still halts when it confronts the nobility of Luxembourg and Jean Jaures and other less celebrated heroes of 1914 - such as the Serbian Dimitri Tucovic.) I came to all these discoveries, and later ones such as the magnificent Regeneration trilogy composed by Pat Barker, through a door that had been forced open for me by Owen's *Dulce Et Decorum Est.*"

All the more ironic then, that in the aftermath of September 11th Hitchens has apparently turned his back on the tradition of Zimmerwald and Rosa Luxembourg, preferring instead to accuse opponents of the War on Terrorism of being 'soft on fascism' in an article in The Spectator: a magazine which has in its time given refuge to every rightward moving crank from Kingsley Amis to Woodrow Wyatt.

A little further on in the foreword Hitchens points out that:

"Many of the writers discussed here have no 'agenda' of any sort, or are conservatives whose insight and integrity I have found indispensable. I remember for example sitting with Jorge Luis Borges in Buenos Aires as he employed an almost Evelyn Waugh-like argument in excusing the military dictatorship that then held power in his country. But I had a feeling that he couldn't keep up this pose, and not many years later he wrote a satirical poem ridiculing the Falklands/Malvinas adventure while also making statements against the junta's cruelty in the matter of the *desaparecidos*. It wasn't just another author signing a letter about 'human rights'; it was the ironic mind refusing the dictates of the literal one."

This sort of talk will probably sound fairly alien to most left-wing activists, brought up as most of them (us) have been on a diet of Ken Loach good, *Brideshead Revisited* bad.

And yet it is far closer to Marx's actual approach to literature - Borges perhaps being a kind of latter-day Argentinean Balzac - than anything you're likely to read in a old issue of *Militant*. A little more commonplace is Hitchens' observation that:

"In the case of the United States, we await a writer who can summon every nerve to cleanse the country of the filthy stain of the death penalty... there is as yet no Blake or Camus or Koestler to synthesise justice and reason with outrage; to compose the poem or novel - as did Herman Melville with flogging in his *White-Jacket* - that will constitute the needful moral legislation."

Of course the well-meaning sentiments are undoubtedly already there, indeed are probably ten-a-penny at every open-mike poetry night from Greenwich Village to San Francisco, but the trick is to combine the political and the aesthetic; to accomplish the usually impossible task of making a statement which as well as being 'true' is memorable to the point of being in some sense beautiful.

The writers with whom Hitchens engages here range from the predictable - George Orwell, Raymond Williams, Gore Vidal, Salman Rushdie and Oscar Wilde - to those such as F. Scott Fitzgerald and Roald Dahl whose work might superficially seem to be almost entirely devoid of political content. *Rebel in Evening Clothes* is the title of a lovely essay on Dorothy Parker who, as a daughter of the massively wealthy Rothschild family and fashion writer for *Vogue*, was perhaps an unlikely radical. And yet her 1919 poem, originally titled *Hate Song* is something which, with the possible exception of a slightly disparaging reference to milkmen, even the most hardened Socialist Realist would surely have to appreciate:

... the Boss;
He made us what we are to-day, -
I hope he's satisfied.
He has some bizarre ideas
About his employees getting to work
At nine o'clock in the morning -
As if they were a lot of milkmen.
He has never been known to see you
When you arrive at 8.45,
But try to come in at a quarter past ten
And he will always go up in the elevator with you.
He goes to Paris on the slightest provocation
And nobody know why he has to stay there so long.

There are also some hilarious demolition jobs; on the horribly glib Tom Wolfe (essayist and author of the novel *Bonfire of the Vanities*); on Tom Clancy (author of *The Hunt for Red October* etc. etc.) whom Hitchens aptly describes as: 'the junk supplier of surrogate testosterone'; and best of all on the prominent American critic Norman Podhoretz of whom he says: 'But as the years passed... Podhoretz began to fawn more openly on Richard Nixon and the Israeli general staff as if rehearsing for the engulfing, mandible-straining blow job he would later bestow on Ronald Reagan.' Of course, in the light his own post-September 11th descent into pro-imperialist jingoism, it is entirely possible that, for Hitchens himself, that particular sentence might yet turn out to be the Ghost of Christmas Yet To Come.

However, the best essay in the entire book is his examination of the life and poetry of Philip Larkin. Ever since the publication of his Selected Letters in 1992 showed that, he was to put it mildly a reactionary and a racist, critical responses to Larkin have tended to polarise into two distinct camps. On the left are those who claim that the fact that Larkin enclosed the following charming little ditty in a letter to a friend, clearly exposes him as the disgusting reactionary they always suspected him of being:

Prison for the strikers
Bring back the cat
Kick out the niggers
How about that?

And for Larkin's critics this is where the case for the prosecution usually rests. Meanwhile his apologists such as the critic John Bailey have claimed that Larkin was simply: 'more free of cant - political, social or literary than any of his peers'. The current Poet Laureate Andrew Motion has even gone so far as to say: 'that Larkin's work had the capacity to create a recognisable and democratic vision of contemporary society.'

Hitchens cuts through both hypocrisy and hyperbole with great skill, providing us with pretty damning evidence that, far from being just another Tory Little Englander, Larkin was in fact a 'frustrated fascist', who after 1945 was forced by the new political realities to hide his real political beliefs; and yet at the same time Hitchens still manages to separate the poems themselves from the political views of the poet:

"unless we lose all interest in contradiction - we are fortunate in being able to say that Larkin's politics are buried well beneath, and somewhere apart from, his poems. The place he occupies in popular affection - which he had won for himself long before the publication of his fouler private thoughts - is the place that he earned, paradoxically, by attention to ordinariness, to quotidian suffering and to demotic humour. Decaying communities, old people's homes, housing estates, clinics... he mapped these much better than most social democrats, and he found words for experience."

Unacknowledged Legislation: Writers In The Public Sphere is a truly excellent book: a must for anyone who has ever complained about one of those left-press reviews in which the reviewer typically uses the last sentence to earnestly inform us that the 'fundamental flaw' in this or that book or film is that nowhere does it provide the working class with an answer to the problems they face under capitalism. The recent political statements of its author, Christopher Hitchens, are, of course, disappointing in the extreme; but they are also perhaps just a contemporary example of the relationship between literature and politics in all its complexity.

February, 2002

GEORGE ORWELL: ANYTHING BUT A SAINT

This year's centenary of George Orwell's birth at Motihari in Bengal, India on 25th June 1903 has seen a marked upturn in interest in both his writing and in the man himself. Penguin have republished pretty much everything he ever wrote - both novels and non-fiction - in a series of glossy volumes, which basically add up to a collected works. There have also been two new biographies, both of which have, to varying degrees, tended to try and shift the spotlight away from George Orwell, the stubborn teller of inconvenient political and social truths, and onto Eric Blair the man behind the pseudonym. There is certainly something to be said for this sort of approach: as someone who has read Orwell's work voraciously over the years I know that I certainly relished the opportunity to leaf through the grubby details of his life. But it also has its limitations.

The fact that he visited prostitutes, made throwaway comments insulting gay contemporaries such as W.H. Auden and didn't like Scottish people is, of course, on one level all very interesting. On another level though it is also completely irrelevant, doing nothing to diminish his critiques of capitalism and Stalinism in works such as *Homage To Catalonia, Road To Wigan Pier, Animal Farm* & *Nineteen Eighty Four*. I once heard someone say that everything Karl Marx had ever written could be dismissed as "rubbish" because he had throughout his life failed to properly provide for his family and (if that wasn't bad enough) then got his housekeeper, Helen Demuth, pregnant. If we were to use, for example, the fact that Orwell apparently sometimes paid for sex to try and in anyway diminish his achievement as a writer and political thinker, then this is the rather intellectually limited road we'd be heading down.

George Orwell was certainly flawed, both as a man and as writer. When he came back to England in 1927, after a five year stint as a Colonial Policeman in Burma, and decided to 'become a writer' he looked like an unpromising wannabe indeed. The poet Ruth Pitter was a neighbour of his at the time:

"He wrote so badly. He had to teach himself writing. He was like a cow with a musket. I remember one story that never saw the light of day... it began 'Inside the park, the crocuses were out...' Oh dear, I'm afraid we did laugh, but we knew he was kind because he was good to our old sick cat."

Like most fledgling writers he started off by writing reams of grandiose garbage. According to Bernard Crick's 1980 biography, *George Orwell: A Life*, the worst of this appears to have been a fragment of a play about a couple whose baby is dying because they can't afford an operation she desperately needs. Despite their desperate need for money Francis, the father, refuses a job "writing advertising copy for 'Pereira's Surefire Lung Balm...' because the firm are swindling crooks, the substance is noxious, and, besides, he's got his artistic integrity to consider.

When his wife reminds him of Baby's needs, he suggests that for her to prostitute herself would be no worse than the job she wants him to take. Then the scenario turns abruptly from naturalism to expressionism... 'Everything goes dark, there is a sound like roaring waters... the furniture is removed' and we are in a timeless prison cell, in something like the French Revolution, with POET, POET'S WIFE and CHRISTIAN who sits reading a large book. He has a placard inscribed DEAF around his neck.

If a contemporary version of this early Orwell lived around the corner from me, I have no doubt that I would spend a good deal of time desperately trying to avoid him. I have known such people and they rarely grow up to produce masterpieces!

The early Orwell's politics were similarly unfocused and adolescent. Looking back on his earlier self from the vantage point of 1936 he has this to say in *The Road To Wigan Pier*:

"I wanted to submerge myself, to get right down among the oppressed; to be one of them against their tyrants. And, chiefly because I had to think everything out in solitude, I had carried my hatred of oppression to extraordinary lengths. At that time [roughly 1928-1933] failure seemed to me to be the only virtue. Every suspicion of self-advancement, even to the extent of making a few hundreds a year, seemed to me spiritually ugly, a species of bullying."

The early Orwell's stance could in a sense be read as the oh so predictable, immature rejection of bourgeois society by one of its more privileged members, who almost certainly only had a vague notion of what the word 'bourgeois' actually meant and certainly hadn't the faintest idea how things might actually be changed. Most such middle-class radicals end up being reabsorbed by the society they once supposedly despised. At best they become concerned journalists or perhaps panellists on *The View*. At worst they end their days thinking that Eoghan Harris has a point. But Orwell was clearly different. His rebellion was a serious one. It was this failure-worshipping stance that led Orwell to drift down among the tramps and winos of London and Paris. And from this milieu came the material for his first book *Down And Out In Paris And London*, published in 1933. By now his writing had greatly improved from those early, laughable efforts. The plain documentary prose style for which he became famous was already visible. Orwell was nothing if not persistent.

In Ruth Pitter's words:

"he had the gift, he had the courage, he had the persistence to go on in spite of failure, sickness, poverty, and opposition"

The three years that followed saw him produce a novel each year, *Burmese Days* (1934), *A Clergy Man's Daughter* (1935) & *Keep The Aspidistra Flying* (1936).

The most significant of these for us is probably *Burmese Days*, a damning anti-imperialist indictment of British colonial rule in Burma: something Orwell knew from the inside having spent five years working as a policeman for the British regime there. All of these novels deal with issues important to Orwell: repression, snobbery, hypocrisy, the worship of money and the frustration of artistic ambitions.

My personal favourite is *Keep The Aspidistra Flying*: his grim but often hilarious portrait of Gordon Comstock, a down-at-heel poet forever beset by financial embarrassment and sexual frustration. Comstock is obsessed with not being ruled by the 'Money God', and so leaves a well paying job writing slogans for an advertising agency, and gets a badly paying job in a bookshop. At least that way he has some hope of retaining his integrity. In the end though his girlfriend, Dorothy, becomes pregnant, and Comstock leaves the bohemian life behind, surrendering himself entirely to a future of Money, Marriage and Aspidistra Plants: all the things he previously spat venom at. Orwell's portrait of Gordon Comstock is perhaps the last we see of his early, unfocussed radicalism. *Keep The Aspidistra Flying* was published in January, 1936. By December of that year the Spanish Civil War had broken out, and Orwell was in Barcelona fighting against the forces of General Franco as a member of the POUM militia.

Just after he'd finished *Keep The Aspidistra Flying* Orwell was commissioned by Victor Gollancz of the Stalinist leaning Left Book Club to write a book of documentary non-fiction about the condition of the unemployed in the industrial north of England. Gollancz offered him an advance of £500, huge money for the time. This was the coincidence which finally pushed George Orwell to become the overtly political writer we have come to know. Years later his friend, Richard Rees, recalled:

"There was such an extraordinary change both in his writing and, in a way also, in his attitude after he'd been to the North and written that book. I mean, it was almost as if there'd been a kind of fire smouldering in him all his life which sudden broke into flame at that time."

Of course events external to Orwell's day to day life played their part too. 1936 was the year when the political and economic crisis of the 1930s really began to seriously gather speed as it hurtled towards disaster and the Second World War. In March of that year the German army moved into the previously demilitarised Rhineland: the first serious violation by Hitler of the Versailles Treaty. On May 1st Italy invaded Abyssinia and Mussolini declared that a new Roman Empire had been established. In July General Franco's forces rose up and tried to overthrow the Republican government in Spain. When they didn't achieve the easy victory they'd expected, the Civil War began. In October Oswald Mosley's Blackshirts were beaten off the streets by anti-fascists at Cable Street as they tried to march through the predominantly Jewish areas of the

East End of London. And in December the abdication of Edward VIII did its bit to heighten the sense of crisis.

When he asked Orwell to write the book that would become *The Road To Wigan Pier*, Victor Gollancz hoped Orwell would produce a book something like *Down And Out In Paris And London*, except that this time the focus would be industrial workers (both employed and unemployed) and their families, rather than tramps. What Orwell actually produced was a book of two very distinct halves: the first of which provides us with some of the best portraits to be found of working class life in 1930s England. For the first time Orwell begins to see working class people as human beings fully conscious of their own position at the bottom of society. In his Wigan Pier diary he recalls watching a young woman trying to unblock a drain with a stick:

"I thought how dreadful a destiny it was to be kneeling in the gutter in a back-alley in Wigan, in the bitter cold, prodding a stick up a blocked drain. At that moment she looked and caught my eye, and her expression was as desolate as I have ever seen; it struck me that she was thinking just the same thing I was."

Elsewhere though his view of working class life is just a little sentimental: "In a working-class home - I am not thinking at the moment of the unemployed, but of comparatively prosperous homes - you breath a warm, decent, deeply human atmosphere which is not so easy to find elsewhere... on winter evenings when the fire glows in the open range and dances mirrored in the steel fender, when Father, in his shirtsleeves, sits in the rocking chair at one side of the fire reading the racing finals, and Mother sits the other with her sewing, and the children with a pennorth of mint humbugs, and the dog lolls roasting himself on the mat..."

The picture Orwell paints of this happy, simple life is so idyllic that it sounds almost like something from a speech by Ronald Reagan or Eamon DeValera. I have to confess that whenever I actually come across people as apparently wholesome as this, I tend to suspect that they either have bodies buried under the patio, or that Father (God bless him) will in the fullness of time be escorted into the back of a police van with a bag over his head, having been caught bouncing the little ones on his knee just a little too vigorously.

The second part of *The Road To Wigan Pier* is a hilarious, if at times slightly cranky portrayal of the organised left of the time. On his way to attend the Independent Labour Party Summer School at Letchworth, Orwell spots two other likely attendees:

"both about sixty, both very short, pink and chubby, and both hatless. One of them was obscenely bald, the other had long grey hair bobbed in Lloyd George style.

They were dressed in pistachio-coloured shirts and khaki shorts into which their huge bottoms were crammed so tightly that you could study every dimple. Their appearance created a mild stir of horror on the top of the bus. The man next to me, a commercial traveller I should say, glanced at me, and then, back at them again, and murmured, 'Socialists'."

Orwell seems to have enjoyed the company of those working-class activists he met in the North of England. But he quite clearly detested those on the left he saw as middle-class trendies or frauds of any type.

" 'Socialism' calls up, on the one hand, a picture of aeroplanes, tractors and huge glittering factories of glass and concrete; on the other, a picture of vegetarians with wilting beards, of Bolshevik commissars (half gangster, half gramophone), of earnest ladies in sandals, shockheaded Marxists chewing polysyllables, escaped Quakers, birth-control fanatics and Labour Party backstairs-crawlers. Socialism, at least in this island, does not smell any longer of revolution and the overthrow of tyrants; it smells of crankiness, machine-worship and the stupid cult of Russia. Unless you remove that smell, and very rapidly, Fascism may win."

Despite his scathing portrayal of much of the left, Orwell himself was nevertheless moving sharply to the left politically. In early December he put the finishing touches to *The Road To Wigan Pier* and made arrangements to travel to Spain, where the civil war was now raging. He arrived in Barcelona on December 22nd and was greatly impressed by what he saw:

"The Anarchists were still in virtual control of Catalonia and the revolution was still in full swing... Practically every building of any size had been seized by the workers and was draped with red flags or with the red and black flags of the Anarchists. Every shop and cafe had an inscription saying that it had been collectivised, even the bootblacks had been collectivised and their boxes painted red and black. Waiters and shop-walkers looked you in the face and treated you as an equal. Servile and even ceremonial forms of speech had temporarily disappeared. Nobody said 'Senor' or 'Don' or even 'Usted'; everyone called everyone else 'Comrade' and 'Thou', and said 'Salud' instead of 'Buenos dias'."

Despite the fact that his experience in Spain would lead Orwell to write what is arguably his best book, *Homage To Catalonia*, during his time there Orwell was more than merely another literary tourist: he fought and was shot and badly injured. It was Orwell's personal experience of the role played by the Stalinists in undermining and ultimately sabotaging this revolution that turned his fairly vague suspicions about 'the cult of Russia' into an implacable hostility towards Stalinism, which he retained for the rest of his life.

During the Russian-backed crackdown on 'Trotsky-Fascist Fifth Columnists' in June 1937 he himself was forced to go on the run, sleeping rough on the streets of Barcelona for several nights, to avoid being rounded up because of his membership of the anti-Stalinist POUM militia. His friend George Kopp was imprisoned and tortured by the Stalinists. The torture with rats of Winston Smith in room 101 in *Nineteen Eighty Four* is apparently partly based on Kopp's treatment at their hands. And yet despite this tragic outcome Orwell left Spain inspired with an impatient, nagging hope:

"For months past we had been telling ourselves that 'when we get out of Spain' we would go somewhere beside the Mediterranean and be quiet for a little while and perhaps do a little fishing ... It sounds like lunacy but the thing that both of us wanted was to be back in Spain. I have recorded some of the outward events, but I suppose I have failed to convey more than a little of what those months in Spain mean to me... the mountain dawns stretching away into inconceivable distances, the frosty crackle of bullets, the roar and glare of bombs; the clear cold light of the Barcelona mornings, and the stamp of boots in the barrack yard, back in December when people still believed in the revolution"

I think it is fair to say that Orwell left Spain a convinced revolutionary socialist. Indeed he spent the next couple of years waiting for a revolution, which in the end didn't come. His next novel *Coming Up For Air* (1939) is a portrait of George Bowling "a fat insurance salesman worn down by a loveless marriage, the expense of a family, children who despise him". Bowling is exactly the sort of beleaguered Mister Average that Orwell thought the left needed to appeal to if it was ever to successfully take power in Britain. The coalminers and the cranks would never be enough.

A win on the horses inspires Bowling to leave home one day and try to recapture something of his youth:

"Of course, his journey is doomed - the small town [where Bowling grew up] had been engulfed by suburbia and his woodland paradise infested with fruit juice drinking, nudist vegetarians, and Garden City cranks... Katie, his childhood sweetheart is now a worn-out, middle-aged drab and the secret pool, the symbolic centre of his childhood fantasy, turned into a rubbish dump. The horrors of the mass society have overwhelmed the holy places and Doomsday threatens in the form of Hitler, Stalin and their streamlined battalions. George returns to his bourgeois prison to face again his nagging wife and unlovable children."

Orwell had clearly moved a long way since the days when he believed that salvation could only be found down among penniless tramps. He was now thinking in concrete terms about how society might actually be changed, and Socialism made to appeal to both the working and middle classes.

The two novels that followed before his premature death from TB in 1950, are what transformed him from a medium-sized 1930s figure into a literary superstar, whose books will no doubt still be read two hundred years from now. *Animal Farm* (1945) is an ingenious Swiftian satire on the Russian Revolution betrayed. Orwell has been accused by some of jumping on the Cold War bandwagon, and of allowing his work to be used by reactionaries and war-mongers to attack the Socialism which he himself believed in.

It's important to remember though that when Orwell was writing and trying to find a publisher for *Animal Farm* the Second World War was still on, and Britain, the United States and the Soviet Union were still allies. Orwell actually found it incredibly difficult to find a publisher for what was seen at the time as another trouble-making book by him. So the charge of opportunism really doesn't stick. Later, Disney (with a little help from the CIA) purchased the film rights to the book and famously removed the last scene in which the animals peer in the window at the pigs and the humans having dinner together, and cannot see any difference between them. Orwell's message that the Stalinist bureaucracy (represented by pigs) and the capitalist class (represented by the humans) were as bad as each other was no doubt a little inconvenient for the American cold war propagandists who hijacked his work. The manner in which lifelong Soviet *apparatchiks* such as Boris Yeltsin and Vladimir Putin managed to transform themselves into advocates of the gangster capitalism now prevalent in Russia shows that he was of course right: in the last analysis there was very little difference between them and the capitalist class in the west. They would do anything to hang onto their positions, up to and including the complete restoration of capitalism.

His last major work was *Nineteen Eighty Four*, a deeply pessimistic portrait of a totalitarian society, resembling those that then existed in Eastern Europe. By the time he wrote this book, Orwell had moved away from the near Marxist stance of *Homage To Catalonia*. His revolutionary moment bad passed. And of course world events had moved on too. The Second World War was over, and Britain now had a Labour government which Orwell basically supported. It was this Labour government - a government far to the left of that of Tony Blair - which created the National Health Service and the Welfare State. By the time Orwell died in 1950, the political situation was completely different to that of 1936: the year he went to fight Spain. Orwell had an instinctive rather than a theoretical attitude to politics. His contempt for theoreticians - "shock-haired Marxist chewing polysyllables" - led him to spend a lot of time reacting against other people's ideas rather than coming up with credible ideas of his own.

The worst example of this is his stance in relation to World War II. In September 1938, during the Czechoslovakia crisis, Orwell published a short article in *New Leader*, the paper of the ILP, in which he stated:

"We repudiate… all appeals to the people to support a war which would, in fact, maintain and extend imperialist possessions and interest, whatever the incidental occasion."

At the time the Stalinist parties where promoting the Popular Front policy. 'Democracy not Fascism' was the slogan and they were desperate to build an alliance against Nazi Germany between the Soviet Union and western powers, such as Britain and France. When the war actually came both Orwell and the Stalinists did a complete about turn. The Hitler/Stalin pact was signed and the Soviet Union stayed out of the war until it was attacked itself in 1941. The Communist Parties attacked the war as 'imperialist', just as Orwell had in his *New Leader* article, while Orwell, on the other hand, strongly supported the war effort and vehemently attacked the anti-imperialist, antiwar point of view, which he himself had still supported as late as August 1939. He never properly explained this about turn. A likely explanation is that, by then, his hatred of the Stalinists was so intense that when he heard them saying one thing, he would, if at all possible say the opposite.

His hatred of all things Soviet was also his motivation, when on May 2nd 1949 he sent a list of suspected Communists and fellow-travellers to the British intelligence services. The list included both literary figures such Stephen Spender and J.B. Priestley, and Labour MPs such as Ian Mikardo and Tom Driberg. A number of the people named by Orwell were outed not just as suspected Communist sympathisers but also as homosexuals. Given that homosexual acts between men were still illegal in Britain, and would remain so for another twenty years, this was a particularly disgusting thing to have done. Orwell handed MI5 material, which they would no doubt use to blackmail left-wingers and socialists. There is no excuse for this.

Despite his many faults though, Orwell is a writer whose work will always be of interest to socialists, indeed to thinking people everywhere. Yes, he was often cranky, often wrong. But his dogged pursuit of the awkward questions of his time led him to produce two of the masterpieces of socialist literature, *Homage To Catalonia* and *Animal Farm*. And the bravery he showed in opposing Stalinism - not when it was weak and collapsing but at the height of its power - cannot be lightly dismissed. If this Orwell lived around the corner from me, he would be welcome to come around for a cup of tea anytime. No doubt we would argue. But such is life.

December, 2003

EVERYTHING THE PARTY DID, SAID AND THOUGHT

a review of *Koba the Dread* by Martin Amis (Jonathan Cape £16.99 stg (hardback))

At the outset I should say that this is one of the most idiosyncratic books I've read in a long time. On one level it is simply a continuation of British novelist Martin Amis's attempt to work out his relationship with his father, Kingsley, who died in 1991. Also a prominent literary figure in his time, Kingsley Amis is perhaps best known for his novel *Lucky Jim* (1954). Its hero Jim Dixon, a lower-middle-class radical whose aggressive anti-establishment, anti-pretension stance led some to associate Kingsley Amis with the group of 1950s British novelists and playwrights usually referred to as the Angry Young Men. And while Kingsley Amis himself always resisted being associated with that particular grouping, he certainly shares much in common with them.

Like most of the Angries he started out as a left-wing radical (a member of the Communist Party from 1941-1956) and ended up somewhere to the right of Margaret Thatcher, whom he adored despite being disappointed that she never actually got around to shooting striking miners or sending the blacks back to Africa. Such minor frustrations aside, Kingsley Amis apparently ended his days relatively content with the general direction in which the world was headed. In his last book *Experience* (published in 2001) Martin Amis investigated his personal relationship with his father. Here he talks about his politics, taking issue, as one would perhaps expect, not with his later lurch to right, but with his earlier support for Stalin.

On one side we have the rather pampered Martin, utterly incapable of imagining for even five minutes a world fundamentally different from that which he sees around him. In many ways Martin Amis is the prototype post-cold war 'liberal'. Concerned, but not too concerned. The closest he's ever come to having a big idea is probably his belief in Tony Blair. Indeed, on page four Amis tells us that he began writing this book "a day or two" after spending the evening of 31st December 1999 at the Millennium Dome in London "along with Tony Blair and the Queen". He had apparently "recently read yards of books about the Soviet experiment."

On the other side we have his cranky father, Kingsley, talking about the loss he felt at letting go of his socialist beliefs:

'The Ideal of the brotherhood of man, the building of the Just City, is one that cannot be discarded without lifelong feelings of disappointment and loss.'

Now, this is a feeling which every disappointed socialist must at some time have felt. Once the possibility of a New Society has raised itself seriously in your head, then there really is no going back. As a friend of mine puts it: "whatever you do you can never unlearn all you now know to be wrong with the world. You can never just get on with things in the same way again."

When one thinks of it this way, it suddenly becomes rather less surprising that so many former revolutionaries end their days as monumental cranks, obsessively spitting poison at anything that even vaguely reminds them of what they themselves once were.

Now, if Martin Amis had restricted himself to writing about the obvious dichotomy between his father's politics and his own, then it could have made for an interesting, if not exactly earth-shattering, little read. Instead, he insists on addressing what the book's jacket blurb describes as: "the central lacuna of twentieth century thought: the indulgence of communism by intellectuals of the West.". If Amis had at his disposal the intellectual equipment to deal properly with the issues involved, that would be one thing. But it so clearly isn't his area. In places he ends up sounding like a loud-mouthed student berating a Trotskyist newspaper-seller outside Trinity College. We are told that, among other things:

'Trotsky was a murdering bastard and a fucking liar... He was a nun-killer - they all were.'

Surely, deep down, a writer of Amis's stature must realise that behind the failure of language explicit in such crude phraseology as "murdering bastard" and "fucking liar" lies a much more important failure of ideas? He can't quite prove his point, so he resorts instead to shouting abuse and stamping his feet. Later we are told of Lenin's reaction to the famine which struck Czarist Russia in 1891:

"He [Lenin] 'had the courage' as a friend put it: to come out and say openly that famine would have numerous positive results... Famine, he explained, in destroying the outdated peasant economy, would... usher in socialism... Famine would also destroy faith not only in the tsar, but in God too".

Clearly this 'friend' of Lenin's was a nineteenth century version of the sort of sad anorak who can sometimes still be found wandering around the fringes of the various far left organisations. You know the sort, the one with slightly mad stare who thinks that what we really need to stir the masses into action is a sudden economic collapse followed immediately by a good long war. The key point here though is that the words belong not to Lenin, but to this unnamed 'friend'. If Amis wanted to convict Lenin of the crime of being indifferent to famine, then he really should have gone to the trouble of finding a quote from the man himself, rather than relying on such dodgy hearsay. It is true that Lenin believed that many of the famine relief schemes of the time were more about appearance than they were about reality:

"In the regional capital of Samara only one intellectual, a twenty-two- year-old lawyer, refused to participate in the effort - and, indeed, publicly denounced it. This was Lenin".

However, there's nothing very surprising about this. For example, there were many - and by no means all of them revolutionary socialists - who thought that the 1985 Live Aid concert was at least as much about ageing rock-stars in general (and Bob Geldof in particular) salving their consciences and using the issue to get publicity for themselves, as it was about the Ethiopian famine. Surely what Lenin said back in 1891 amounted to nothing more than a nineteenth century Russian version of the same thing?

Marxists are often accused, sometimes correctly so, of crude reductionist thinking. And yet here it is Amis who is desperate to simplistically collapse complex issues together. Marx is glibly dismissed as "a long dead German economist whose ideas [in the 1970s] were bringing biblical calamity to China, North Korea, Vietnam, Laos and Cambodia." Marxism = Stalinism. End of story. No mention of the fact that nowadays even many Wall Street economists regularly refer to the works of this 'long dead German economist'. To admit such an inconvenient fact would be to allow a shade of grey. And in this book Amis works only in black and white.

He makes no real attempt to differentiate between Stalinism and Trotskyism, preferring instead to pretend that they are one and the same thing. He asks his friend, the prominent British poet and one time Trotskyist, James Fenton: "How he... could align himself with a system that saw literature as a servant of the state; and, I thought, [you] must hate the language, the metallic clichés, the formulas and euphemisms". There is a vast reservoir of non-Stalinist Marxist literary criticism into which Amis could have dipped, if he was even slightly interested in getting a real answer to this question. But why bother with nuance, when caricature will do? Similarly, he tells another friend (and former Trotskyist), the essayist and critic Christopher Hitchens, that: "An admiration for... Trotsky is meaningless without an admiration for terror. [He] would not want your admiration without an admiration for terror. Do you admire terror?" It is as if the victims of the show trials of 1936 and 1938, such as Trotsky, Kamenev, Bukharin and Zinoviev, were as guilty as those who tortured and murdered them. Amis again and again accuses Marxists of being glib about human suffering, only to end up being very glib about it himself.

As far as I'm concerned anyone who supported, or acted as an apologist for, regimes such as those in the Soviet Union, Eastern Europe, China and North Korea certainly has questions to answer. In case anyone out there needs reminding of just how rough it sometimes got in the so-called 'socialist' countries, here is a description of life in the Gulag:

"A group of prisoners at Kolyma were hungry enough to eat a horse that had been dead for more than a week (despite the stench and the infestation of flies and maggots). Scurvy makes the bones brittle; but then, 'Every prisoner welcomes a broken arm or leg.' Extra-large scurvy boils were 'particularly envied'.

Admission to hospital was managed by quota. To get in with diarrhoea, you had to be evacuating (bloodily) every half hour. A man chopped off half his foot to get in there. And prisoners cultivated infections, feeding saliva, pus or kerosene to their wounds".

I personally would find it difficult to take very seriously anyone who ever so much as whispered an excuse for a regime such as this. Yes, we all make mistakes. But there are mistakes. And then again there are *mistakes*. However, there are, of course, also those on the Left who never believed that the Soviet Union was any sort of paradise. The problem now is that we have all, to some extent, been painted with the same brush. To most people Marxism now either means failure or it means North Korea. And as soon as your average Joe and Josephine start thinking about North Korea, you can be sure it won't be long before they're also thinking how George W. Bush isn't so bad after all.

Yes, *Koba The Dread* is in many ways an absurd book; so deficient that had its author not already been very famous, it would probably never have been accepted for publication by a reputable publisher. But in one sense that is neither here nor there. The real issue is what, if anything, the Left can do to disentangle itself from Stalin's legacy? A few glib sentences here and there about North Korea being either 'state-capitalist' or a 'deformed workers' state' are unlikely to be enough. The thing which above all else fatally undermined the revolutionary left in the 20th Century was the disastrous knack it developed - and I think some of the Trotskyist organisations are probably guilty here as well - of turning generation after generation of wide-eyed young activists into grim apologists for everything the Party did, said and thought. If the word 'socialism' is to have any relevance at all in the 21st Century, then this is surely the issue which, above all else, must be addressed.

February, 2003

TWENTY YEARS AGO TODAY
David Peace. *GB 84* Faber and Faber, 462 pages, E19. 50.

This time twenty years ago the miners' strike was raging. The morning radio news was full of flying pickets and pitched battles between miners and police; the evening television dominated by images of the same. Names of places such as Cortonwood, Ollerton and Orgreave were burned into the consciousness forever, simply because we heard them so often. Cortonwood, where it all started when the National Coal Board announced the Yorkshire pit's arbitrary closure in the first week of March 1984. (Within days it became clear that this was part of a much larger pit-closure programme.) Ollerton, the Nottinghamshire mining village where the strike claimed its first fatality, when a young miner was killed in a crush between pickets and police during the second week of the strike. Orgreave, the Yorkshire coking plant then vital to Britain's electricity supply, where the miners tried to repeat their famous 1972 victory, when they succeeded in closing down a similar plant at Saltley, Birmingham by mass picketing. This time it didn't work.

The miners were lured to Orgreave from South Wales, Kent, Durham, Yorkshire, Scotland and elsewhere in their tens of thousands on a beautiful June day to face the massed power of the British state: thousands of police with horses, dogs and riot gear ready, willing and able to turn the miners back. From that day on we all knew something had changed. This wasn't 1972 or 74. There'd be no easy victory. And in the end, which didn't come until March 1985 - a whole year after the strike started - there was no victory at all. The miners went back without a settlement, their union's power broken, their industry about to be destroyed.

David Peace's novel *GB84*, which he describes as "a fiction, based on fact", charts the course of the strike from the optimism of the early days, through the pitched battles of the summer to the slowly dawning reality of total defeat. Peace uses a traditional, linear narrative structure interspersed with extracts from the diaries of two miners, Martin and Peter. And much of the time it works. Younger readers for whom it has only ever been ancient history would certainly get at least an idea what the miners strike was like.
Peace writes in an accessible style, without in any sense trying to dumb complex issues down. And he provides us with more than the bare documentary facts. Indeed, *GB 84* brings that apocalyptic year more credibly back to life than many an earnest but dead-in-the-mouth speech at many a far-left meeting. It makes the strike human again by giving the reader a real sense of the emotions it stirred, as the high hopes of activists and trade unionists everywhere turned so bitterly into their opposite.

GB84 is divided into five chapters, each of which has a title of its own; the first four - 'Ninety-nine red balloons', 'Two Tribes'; 'Careless Whisper' and

'There's a world outside your window and it's a world of dread and fear' - are all references to popular songs of the time. No doubt some will complain that Peace is trivialising such a momentous event by naming a chapter in a book about it after a song written by George Michael. (I have to say though that for some strange reason I personally have always found it useful to know what was in the charts the year a particular event happened. Knowing, say for example, that T-Rex were in the charts the year Ireland joined the EEC, or that Renée and Renato had their one hit wonder 'Save Your Love' the year the Falklands War happened somehow makes those events seem more rather than less real. Sad, I know. But true.) With the title of the last chapter 'Terminal, or the Triumph of the Will' Peace leaves such frivolity behind, and everything is suddenly deadly serious.

For me, the best writing in the whole novel are the two extracts from Martin's diary in the last chapter. On day 364 of the strike, when more than 50 per cent of the miners have drifted back to work, and the National Conference of the NUM has voted by 98-91 to recommend a return to work without a settlement, Martin summons up the ghosts of all the previous generations of miners whose struggles made the tradition which Thatcher succeeded in decisively trampling into the dirt:

"The Dead that carried us from far to near. Through the villages of the Damned, to stand beside us here. Under their banners and their badges. In their branches and their bands - Their muffled drums. Their muted pipes - That whisper. That echo - Their funeral marches. Their funeral music - That moans. That screams - Again and again. For ever more - As if they are marching their way up out of their graves. Here to mourn the new dead - The country deaf to their laments."

In many ways the tempo of *GB84* resembles that of a symphony, and the extract quoted above is part of its catastrophic crescendo. The black pessimism of the defeated strike is, in a sense, the flip-side of the near hubris of its early days:

"Motion to back strike is proposed. Motion is seconded. Motion is backed 100 per cent - Folk head off to Hotel or Club. Lot of talk about '72 and '74. I'm having a piss in Club when this bloke says to me, it'll be right then? I say, how do you mean? We'll win? He says. Yeah, I tell him. What you worried about?"

Generally speaking, Peace weighs the significance of different events well. One criticism I would have though is that, in a couple of places, his narrative is laced with just a little too much fatalism. Clearly, by Christmas 1984 the miners were doomed. But between March and October it was by no means certain that Thatcher was going to prevail.

Peace downplays the significance of Arthur Scargill's mistake in not calling a national ballot, by having one of his characters - an almost satanic government advisor referred to throughout the book as "the Jew" - talk in March '84 about "the very unlikely event of a national ballot and... even unlikelier event of a vote for strike." Now, this is simply wrong.

All the evidence is that the overwhelming majority of miners and their families supported the strike at this stage. And, if anything, support for the strike increased during the spring and summer as more miners and their wives became more actively involved, and the strike gained the sympathy of a wide coalition of people in every corner of Britain: everyone from traditional trade-unionists to the Sikh community in Birmingham to gay and lesbian groups in London and Brighton. The miners received money collected by sympathisers world-wide; even receiving cheques from such non-proletarian sources as Elizabeth Taylor and, the American billionaire, John Paul Getty.

If there was a national ballot anytime between April and August, when 80 per cent of miners were on strike, it's a racing certainty that the ballot would have endorsed the strike. And this would have given the strike added legitimacy, which would certainly have persuaded many of those in Nottinghamshire and elsewhere, who continued to work, to join the strike. The miners' tradition was to have a national ballot when the issue was national strike action; there were national ballots in both 1972 and 1974. And not to have had one in 1984 was a major strategic error brought about, at least in part, because of the top-down, bureaucratic socialism of Miners' Union President Arthur Scargill. The miners may still not have won if there'd been a ballot, but they would certainly have had a much better chance.

Another window of possibility David Peace downplays a little is the threatened strike action by NACODS, the union which represented pit-deputies, who were responsible for pit safety, and without whom no mine could legally stay open. They voted for strike 82%-18% in October '84. If implemented, this would have meant every working miner in Britain being sent home. After seven months the strike would finally (if only by default) be 100 per cent solid. With a NACODS strike still threatened, Peace has the aforementioned government advisor 'the Jew' confidently ranting:

"there must be no further negotiations. There must be no further promises of no compulsory redundancies. There must be no amnesty and no jobs for any miners convicted of criminal offences. The times have changed..."

At that stage outright victory was probably beyond the miners' grasp, but the likelihood has to be that, if NACODS walked out and stayed out, there would have been some sort of fudge.

Thatcher would not have claimed her famous victory. And everyone would have lived to fight another day. However, the national executive of NACODS called off their strike at the last minute, and the rest is history.

Peace does a good job, though, of illustrating the sheer ruthlessness of the Thatcher government. On page 253 he has 'The Jew', whose actual name is Stephen Sweet, draw up a strategy to entice striking miners back to work:

"The Jew wants a copy of the entire payroll for the National Coal Board. The Jew wants every miner's name checked against police and county court records - The Jew wants weaknesses- Men who have transferred to their pit. Men who live a distance from their pit - Men who are married. Men divorced. Men who have children. Men who can't - Men who have mortgages. Men who have debts - Men who used to work a lot of overtime. Men who used to have a lot of money - Men who have weaknesses. Age. Sex. Drink. Theft. Gambling. Money. The Jew wants lists."

Two things really irritated me about this mostly enjoyable book. The first was the constant reference to this government advisor as 'The Jew'. Only a couple of times in 462 pages is he referred to Stephen Sweet. I could see no reason for this, other than self-indulgence (or perhaps an attempt at sensationalism) on the part of the author. The second was the gangster subplot, which is so obviously a tacked-on afterthought (perhaps designed to widen the book's appeal?) that it's actually possible to read the rest of the book without bothering with the subplot at all.

So, *GB84* is an imperfect book rather than any sort of masterpiece. But it has enough going for it to make it worthwhile. And it obviously has particular significance for those on the Left. It charts the progress of a battle, which in the words of Michael Eaton - the all too real Saatchi & Saatchi advisor appointed by Thatcher to advise the Coal Board - was the "decisive occasion in recent British history when the right won and the left lost." It took some on the left years to come to terms with the gravity of this defeat. When Thatcher resigned six years later, the bulk of her agenda had been carried out. The Miner's Strike was the decisive point when Thatcherism might have been stopped, but wasn't. Her victory ended a long period of heightened class conflict in Britain, which had started with the struggle against the Heath Tory government in the early 1970s; and created in its place a world fit for New Labour and Michael O'Leary of Ryanair. It also allowed Thatcher to become a credible icon for those advocating the restoration of the free market in Eastern Europe. From Poland to Dublin Airport the after-effects of the miners' defeat can still be seen. It was in a sense the event which, more than any other, gave birth to the world we all now live and work in.

PALACES OF MEMORY, ROOMS FULL OF LIGHT
Meaghan Delahunt. *In The Blue House*. Bloomsbury. £6.99 stg (paperback).

Meaghan Delahunt's debut novel – a fictionalised version of Leon Trotsky's last years in Mexico and, in particular, his relationship with the artist Frida Kahlo – bucks a number of the trends which have lately come to dominate the rather precious world of contemporary English language fiction. Given the typically *oh so* self-obsessed novels about getting divorced in Hampstead (A la Martin Amis) or going to find yourself in Spain (A la Colm Tóibín) which currently dominate the bookshelves in Eason's and Waterstones, it was refreshing indeed to find a novel in which history, far from being over, is writ large; and to encounter characters who, for better or for worse, actually mattered in the grand scheme of things. However, perhaps the way this novel differs from most of its contemporaries is best illustrated by the fact that I actually managed to read it from beginning to end – all 304 pages – without once being tempted to see what was on the television. Episode after episode of *Home and Away* and *The Bold and the Beautiful* drifted into oblivion as it grabbed and held my attention.

Delahunt successfully weaves the messy details of Trotsky's personal life (such as the affair with Kahlo and its aftermath) and the tumultuous events of his political life into an impressively seamless whole. To do this she uses an occasionally bewildering variety of narrators, everyone from Trotsky and Kahlo themselves to Stalin, Beria, the poet Mayakovsky and Ramon Mercader, the man who eventually wielded that ice-pick. She also skips around considerably in time. For example, the story 'starts' shortly after Frida Kahlo's death in July 1954 with Señora Rosita Moreno reminiscing about Kahlo's life in the Blue House of the title. On page 175, though, we're suddenly back in 1898 and the young Trotsky is pacing around his first ever prison cell in Odessa. Changing narrator with each chapter, Delahunt's version of the story moves relentlessly back and forth through time before ending back where it began with Frida Kahlo's death in 1954. A structure which in the hands of a less accomplished writer could have made the novel confusing and episodic actually works very well.

The chapters are short and punchy, and almost entirely devoid of self-indulgent first novel rambling. The book apparently evolved from a short story of Delahunt's, *In the Blue House at Coyoacan*, which was published in the Australian literary magazine *Heat* back in 1998. And one gets the impression that it has been through several drafts. Facing into a story like this must have been an absolutely daunting task for a first-time novelist such as Delahunt. To begin with, the fact that it is based on the lives of prominent historical figures, who were alive as recently as the middle of the last century, means that you need more than dramatic tension to keep the reader interested.

Hardly anyone will read on simply to find out 'what happened in the end', because the vast majority of Delahunt's potential readers will already have known at least the basics of the 'Trotsky story' long before they picked up her book. Of course, one definite advantage *In The Blue House* has from the outset is that, quite unlike the typical Hampstead divorcee, its characters are all such interesting people.

It is, above all else, a book about Trotsky's personal reaction to the devastating political defeats he suffered during the last decade and a half of his life. As Delahunt tells it, his affair with Frida Kahlo was something of an attempt to recapture his former glory at a time when, deep down, he knew perfectly well that his days were numbered:

> 'He had seen himself new, had felt as if all the accumulations of his past had been rolled back in the body of a person much younger than himself who knew only the grandeur of him and none of its fading.
> For Natalia [his wife] knew the lustre. She knew, also, the efforts to maintain it, to polish. The effort, sometimes, to keep going.
> The younger woman saw none of this, and this cheered him. Made him forget how much effort it took to rise again in the morning, preparing for battle, wondering if that day would be his last and, if that were the case, how best to live it.'

How different this Trotsky is from the caricature 'Strelnikov' in *Doctor Zhivago* with his deadpan declaration about the personal life being "dead in Russia". Much has been made of the way Trotsky supposedly shrugged off even the most devastating political setbacks. And no doubt he had an amazing capacity for picking himself up and starting from scratch again. However, I have to say that I think Delahunt does us a service by making her Trotsky rather more completely human than the one we are used to. Shortly before his death in August 1940 she has him suffering from insomnia and wondering if he had "like Marx, neglected those closest to him? Made intolerable demands upon them?... Maybe he had no talent for love or intimacy." Some will undoubtedly read these thoughts as belonging more to Delahunt than to Trotsky, and as such will see them as the self-justification of someone who simply hadn't the stomach for the long, hard haul of revolutionary politics. However, this would, I think, be a crude reading to say the least. After all, who among those of us who've had any sort of serious involvement in revolutionary politics has not, on occasion, paused to consider the toll that involvement has taken on their personal life?

My favourite passage, though, is on page 253 in a chapter narrated by Trotsky's wife Natalia:

> 'Of course, later, when personal tragedy consumed us, when we lost everyone [including all of their children]... He would stand at the

window and look up at the moon. He would pack the dead away inside himself. So many spaces for the dead inside. We spoke often of our palaces of memory. In these rooms our children still played. Friends still embraced; we clinked glasses in rooms full of light. But some rooms, after we had endured too much, could never be opened.'

Though this is clearly a description of a deeply personal tragedy, it could also be read as a sustained metaphor for the complete crushing of revolutionary optimism in any time or place. And, while it would certainly be ludicrous to make any direct comparison between the relatively small sacrifices activists today sometimes make and the gothic tragedy which engulfed Trotsky, there are, I think, many of us who know something about what it's like to have long-lost comrades with whom we still occasionally clink glasses in imaginary "rooms full of light". As a former Trotskyist activist herself, Delahunt clearly knows what she's talking about here. However, far from being some dry political tract, *In The Blue House* is, on the contrary, a very accomplished work of art indeed. By avoiding hero worship and, instead, painting this picture of a decidedly fallible Trotsky grappling with the consequences of a catastrophic political defeat, Delahunt succeeds in making him someone the contemporary reader can really believe in.

Summer, 2002

TOO OBVIOUS FOR HIS OWN GOOD

Ruairi Quinn. *Straight Left - A Journey Into Politics*, 411 pages, E30

Once upon a time, in a land of dole queues, moving statues and rotten coffee; when he was Minister for Labour and I was a duffel-coated member of Galway West Labour Youth; hating Ruairi Quinn was one of my favourite pastimes. During the miserable years of the 1982-1987 Fine Gael-Labour Coalition, he seemed to epitomise everything that was wrong with the Irish Labour Party. He was the 'socialist' who could (and did) quote Marx out of one side of his mouth, while out of the other justifying the use of the army to break the 1986 Dublin Corporation refuse workers' strike. If the revolution the teenage me believed was on its way had come to pass, it would have been very bad news indeed for Ruairi Quinn. A friend of mine, also then a member of Galway West Labour Youth, once told me that he thought that, come the revolution, we should start Ruairi Quinn's re-education by making him clean the late lamented Eyre Square public toilets without the aid of a mop, bucket or pair of rubber gloves. I remember thinking that this was perhaps a bit soft. All that said it's been years now since I've given Ruairi Quinn much thought. The therapy is working nicely. And with Pat 'work-permit' Rabbitte opening his mouth as he has been lately, there are clearly other more immediately deserving cases crying out to be dealt with.

I opened this book determined to give Ruairi Quinn a chance, to let him state his case. I was determined, that however difficult it might be, I would listen to what he had to say. Also, it is absolutely possible to profoundly disagree with what someone is saying and at the same time admire the way they say it. To pretend otherwise is to take the first step down the sad path of literary Stalinism. Margaret Thatcher, Ronald Reagan and Adolf Hitler (to name just three) all sometimes had an undeniable way with words. It was one of the things that made each of them, in their different ways, so disastrously effective. This is definitely not the case with Ruairi Quinn. As a writer he is dull beyond belief. The entire book is written in a passionless, pedantic style. The chapter on the aforementioned 1982-87 Coalition Government limps to a conclusion with the sentence: "We were out of government and a general election was not far away." In terms of literary style, that's about as thrilling as it gets. Gore Vidal he is definitely not.

The practical achievement Quinn gets most excited about is the creation of the FAS Community Employment Scheme in January 1993, when he was Minister for Enterprise and Employment in the Fianna Fail-Labour Coalition: "Since its launch 250,000 people have participated in the scheme." There is no doubt that CE schemes are the backbone of many important social and community services around the country; but the only people who actually get full time (and well paid) jobs from these schemes are the managers.

There are no real trade union rights, because if scheme participants complain they won't be kept on for the second year. Surely those who do essential work in Community Resource Centres and Citizen's Information Centres (to name just two) deserve better than this? As it is, CE schemes are often the place where failed trade union bureaucrats and retired Workers Party hatchet-women go to administrate. But then it's hardly surprising that Ruairi Quinn would be proud of a scheme whose ultimate beneficiaries are a few hundred professional form-fillers. It's the sort of thing every podgy social democrat's dreams are made of.

The worst thing about this book, though, is its shaky relationship with the basic facts of Quinn's own political career. In his account of the 1982-87 period, the 1986 Divorce Referendum is not mentioned. This omission is striking because Quinn was a member of the Coalition Government which proposed it. And the introduction of Divorce was meant to be the sort of progressive reform which justified Labour's participation in what turned out to be an extremely unpopular government. It was a crucial part of their strategy. Presumably, it isn't mentioned because its huge defeat (by 65%-35%) makes it an unpleasant fact, and Ruairi Quinn doesn't like unpleasant facts. He far prefers to spend page after page waxing unlyrical about what a great thing FAS is. Also not mentioned is the same Government's decision, in August 1984, to cut by 50% the subsidies on essential food items, such as milk and bread. This was announced on the August bank holiday weekend, at the height of the holiday season, and the FG-Labour Coalition hoped no-one would notice. In reality, there was uproar, and from that day they faced certain electoral doom; though they managed to cling to office for another ghastly two and a half years.

Such obfuscation aside, even when it comes to basic retellings of events he was involved in, Quinn often gets it wrong. On page 181 he says that, when Michael O'Leary resigned as Labour Leader and joined Fine Gael in late 1982, the result of the leadership contest which followed was "two [votes] for Barry [Desmond] and thirteen for Dick [Spring]". This isn't true. The candidate opposing Dick Spring wasn't Barry Desmond but Michael D. Higgins, and the result was twelve for Spring and two for Michael D. On page 175 he has the 1982 Dublin West by-election (a disaster for Labour) take place on the same day as the Galway East by-election, in which they did reasonably well. This isn't true either. The said Dublin West by-election took place on May 11th 1982; while the Galway East by-election took place two months later, in July. I remember this because the Sunday before the Galway East by-election, the Connaught Football Final took place in Tuam, I was there with my dad and all the three main political leaders - Haughey, Fitzgerald and O'Leary — turned up to canvas the crowd afterwards. It was a beautiful day spoiled only by the sight of a small plane dragging a 'Vote Fine Gael' banner across the sky.

Ruairi Quinn is so in love with being able to say whatever he wants, his relationship with fact has been distorted to such an extent that he is probably incapable of telling you the time without factoring in some sort of lie. The more 'successful' Labour Leaders, such as Dick Spring, Tony Blair and (perhaps) Pat Rabbitte, are usually part con-man, part believer in their own propaganda. Ruairi Quinn's ultimate weakness was that, when it came to it, even he couldn't believe a word he said. As a political charlatan he was just a little too obvious for his own good.

February, 2006

STREET BALLET OF THE DEAF AND DUMB: EVERYDAY LIFE IN THE GDR

Stasiland. Stories From Behind The Berlin Wall by Anna Funder. Granta Books, 286 pages, £7.99

This study of life in the German Democratic Republic might at first glance be dismissed as an attempt by a writer-tourist from a relatively comfortable liberal democracy - Funder is Australian - to finish off something that was already dead. Given that everyone this side of North Korea knows the GDR was a miserable police-state; and that its end was ignominious; what more could there be to say about how ghastly life there was? Funder's fascination with the GDR was sparked by a visit to Leipzig in 1994: "East Germany still felt like a secret walled-in Garden, a place lost in time. It wouldn't have surprised me if things tasted differently here - apples like pears, say, or wine like blood."

She begins her quest with a visit to Runde Ecke, the Stasi museum, the building that had previously housed the East German Ministry for State Security. The citizens' committee administering the museum had left all the desks just as they were the night the demonstrators took the building: "frighteningly neat". There were mounted displays on particleboard screens: "My favourites were the pictures of protesters occupying the building on 4 December 1989... As they entered the building, the Stasi guards had asked to see the demonstrators' identity cards, in a strange parody of the control they were, at that very moment, losing. The demonstrators, in shock, obediently pulled their cards from their wallets. Then they seized the building." Given its subject matter *Stasiland* could easily have become, in the hands of a lesser writer, a worthy but grim effort with a core-readership of insomniacs who specialise in dead Stalinist states. But from the outset, Funder's acute awareness of the absurdity that often accompanies the worst tyrannies, saves the book from that. In the museum she finds the following instructions to Stasi agents:

SIGNALS FOR OBSERVATION
1. Watch out! Subject is coming - touch nose with hand or handkerchief
2. Subject is moving on, going further, or overtaking - stroke hair with hand, or raise hat briefly
3. Subject standing still - lay one hand against back, or on stomach
4. Observing Agent wishes to terminate observation because cover threatened - bend and retie shoelaces
5. Subject returning - both hands against back, or on stomach
6. Observing Agent wishes to speak with Team Leader or other Observing Agents - take out briefcase or equivalent and examine contents.

From this she conjures a blackly comic scene, made all the more laughable by the fact that this was supposedly being done in the name of world socialism:

"I pictured the street ballet of the deaf and dumb: agents signalling to each other from corner to corner: stroking noses, tummies, backs and hair, tying and untying shoelaces, lifting their hats to strangers and rifling through papers".

Funder's curiosity about this spy-dominated society (one full-time Stasi officer for every 63 people) is made all the more acute by her perception that many Germans, particularly those from the West, seem determined to forget it. A work colleague of hers at the overseas television service in what was West Berlin tells her in an outburst: "No-one here is interested - they were backward and they were broke, and the whole Stasi thing... It's sort of embarrassing." What really makes this book work is the way Funder leaves, or at least appears to leave, any preconceived ideas she may have had at the door, and allows the people she meets - both the victims and supporters of the old regime - to speak.

The other piece of writing her open approach and deadpan style most calls to mind is Joan Didion's masterpiece essay 'Slouching Towards Bethlehem'. If someone is condemned, then they are condemned mostly by their own words. One of the most exotic characters here is Karl Eduard von Schnitzler, whose job as presenter of *The Black Channel* in the GDR was "to show extracts from western television broadcast into the GDR - anything from news items to game shows to *Dallas* - and rip it to shreds." Funder interviews von Schnitzler and finds him still ranting in the glib, self-righteous way fallen-down apologists for horrible regimes often do. She reads him a long and very bombastic extract from a transcript of one of his broadcasts, which concludes with him saying that the Berlin Wall was "a service to humanity!" But in von Schnitzler's mind he has nothing whatsoever to be sorry about. "When I finish, he's staring at me, chin up. 'And your question young lady?' 'My question is whether today you are of the same view about the Wall as something humane, and the killings on the border an act of peace.' "He raises his free arm, inhales and screams, 'More! Than! Ever!' He brings his fist down."

Like most demagogues, he's a great believer in exclamation marks. Later, von Schnitzler refers to Erich Mielke, Minister of State Security from 1957 until the regime's demise, as "a living example of the most humane human being". When he passed away to his eternal reward in 1999, most of those who'd lived under Mielke's ever watchful eye begged to differ, and the newspaper headlines read: 'Most hated man now dead'. As the closest thing the German Democratic Republic ever had to a television critic, it's perhaps not surprising that von Schnitzler finds time for a rant about the reality TV show *Big Brother*.

However, even when he's taking easy pot-shots at such 'decadent', 'bourgeois' targets, von Schnitzler manages to make western capitalist society at its most Martha Stewart/Brittany Spears venal seem infinitely preferable to any version of his socialist workers republic. The tragedy is that he believes every word of his finger-wagging defence of the GDR. Unlike many younger regime apparatchiks, von Schnitzler didn't originally join the Communist movement out of a wish to make a soft living spying on and brainwashing his neighbours, but for what must have seemed at the time like high principles indeed: "von Schnitzler is one... whose ideas were moulded in the 1920s by the battle against the gross free market injustices of the Weimar Republic and then the outrages of fascism."

Of course, once a political (or religious) movement has convinced itself that it, and it alone, has all of the answers to humanity's problems, then the telling of politically convenient lies and the demonisation of opponents does tend to become institutionalised. And so the lies multiply until the organisation in question [in this case East Germany's ruling Party of Democratic Socialism] has, at best, a semi-detached relationship with reality. If people are afraid to tell you the truth, then you'll never hear it; which is not to say that you'll escape it, as Stalin's children, from Honecker to Ceaucescu, all eventually found out.

Perhaps the saddest story here is that of Miriam from Leipzig and her husband Charlie. Her story begins in 1968, when "the old University Church was demolished suddenly, without any public consultation." A demonstration against the demolition was doused by the police with fire-hoses and arrests were made. Miriam, then 16, and her friend Ursula decided "this was not right" and so proceeded to stick up some leaflets which simply said "Consultation, not water cannon!" and "People of the People's Republic speak up!" This one impetuous teenage act resulted in an eighteen month prison sentence in Stauberg, the women's prison at Hoheneck. After prison Miriam says that she was "basically no longer human".

Over the next 10 years there followed an unsuccessful attempt to scale the Wall, and then the beating to death in custody of her husband, Charlie, which the Stasi went to elaborate lengths to pass off as a suicide. Miriam's story, beautifully written by Funder, is on its own well worth the cover price. It is also a stark reminder that however much some of us on the Left may still find it galling to admit, when US Presidents, from Kennedy to Reagan, stood on the western side of the Berlin Wall and talked about 'liberty' and 'freedom', those words did actually mean something.

October, 2004

THE CONDEMNED APPLE
Albanian poet Visar Zhiti

The Condemned Apple: Selected Poetry by Visar Zhiti, translated by Robert Elsie, and published by Green Integer, is quite simply the most disturbing collection of poetry I've ever read. Visar Zhiti was born on December 2nd 1952 in the port of Durres on the Adriatic coast. Between 1970 and 1973 his first published poems appeared in literary periodicals. By 1973 Visar was preparing his first collection of poems, *Rhapsody of the life of roses*. Pretty standard stuff so far. If he'd lived in Ireland or Britain, Visar might have gone on to be nominated for a Forward Prize or some such, or been invited to showcase his first collection at The Ledbury Festival or Cúirt. Or he might have been ignored, and if this happened he would, no doubt, have complained about it to his friends. Such is the poet's life. At least as we have come to know it.

But Visar Zhiti didn't live in Brighton or Galway, he lived in a country under the absolute rule of the fanatical Stalinist, Enver Hoxha, who made Nicolae Ceaucescu look like a benign liberal. Hoxha was a crank of gargantuan proportions. After first falling out with the Soviet Union, when Khrushchev admitted that Stalin had actually made a mistake or two, Hoxha then proceeded to fall out with the Chinese when, after Mao's death, they called a halt to the so called 'Cultural Revolution' and put the Gang of Four — including Mao's wife Jiang Qing — on trial. He condemned the Soviet Union, the People's Republic of China (and all their satellites from Cuba to North Korea) as "bourgeois revisionists". By the mid-nineteen seventies Albania had broken off diplomatic and economic contact with the rest of the communist world, it was now officially 'the only socialist country in the world'. It was also probably the second worst place in the world to live. In terms of grim Stalinist brutality, only Pol Pot outstrips the Albanian regime.

It was hardly the ideal circumstances in which to be publishing a first collection of poems. Zhiti had just submitted the manuscript of his first collection to the Naim Frasheri publishing company, when the 'Purge of the Liberals' happened at the Plenary Session of the Communist Party in Tirana. That the 'Liberals' in question only existed in Enver Hoxha's imagination was neither here nor there; they had to be purged anyway. And Zhiti suffered as a result. His work was interpreted as "blackening socialist reality". In 1979 two members of the League of Writers and Artists - their names are abbreviated here to R.V. and P.K - prepared an "expert opinion" on the poetic works of Visar Zhiti, at the request of the Ministry of the Interior. The two lackeys dutifully handed over their twelve-page 'expert opinion' to the authorities on October 24th 1979. Two weeks later Visar Zhiti was arrested.

He was finally released on 28th January 1987, having done the rounds of the Albanian gulags, including the hellish copper mines at Spac.

This 'expert opinion' is republished in full at the back of the book. It makes chilling reading, in particular because its vehement denunciation of the "obscure language" and "hermetic" nature of some of Zhiti's poems reminds me of things I've actually heard socialist friends - some of them now former friends - say about the works of poets such as Medbh McGuckian and John Ashbery. Much left wing literary criticism, particularly as it appears in the small-press, is still laced with Stalinist attitudes. These days there are few overt Stalinists left, but there are certainly those on the literary left who talk Trotsky - 'no party line when it come to art', and all that - but act Stalin when dealing with poetry which doesn't appear to serve the cause. Bad and all as things are, those of us who live in the Western world are at least still basically free to write whatever we want. Our poems may languish mostly ignored - that's a different issue - but at least Medbh McGuckian is not in danger of being denounced by the Ministry for the Interior for not being Adrian Mitchell or Linton Kwesi Johnson. Having condemned Visar Zhiti for the obscurity of some of his poems; R.V. and P.K of the League of Writers and Artists then go on to roundly condemn him for clearly saying what they don't want to hear:

"In the poem, 'For Julia', a mountain lass attends university wearing an old army jacket her brother gave her when he finished his military service. The writer's intentions are obvious here. In such poems he is endeavouring to blacken our life and make little of the economic well-being which socialism has brought to all of us, including the inhabitants of the mountains."

The major criticism I would have of this collection is that the offending poems, those referred to in R.V. and P.K's "expert opinion", are not included. It would have been very interesting to read them. The collection is dominated by poems Visar Zhiti 'wrote' during his years in prison. Deprived of writing paper and pencils, he memorised these poems in an attempt to avoid losing his mind. In the translation from the original Albanian to English, much must have been lost. And yet Robert Elsie's translations of Zhiti's poems are powerful and moving. Some of Zhiti's short poems are beautifully accurate, the sharpest perhaps being 'Moments Pass':

Moments pass
Over my body
Like lice

In this hole of a prison
Filled with the soil of suffering
I sit and wait

How sad it is
To be a warrior
       without war
(1982)

In the incredibly stark poem 'The Prison Shower Room', memorised while he was in Qafe-Bari prison camp in July 1983, Zhiti shows how even in the most dreadful circumstances human beings will cling to what small pleasures they can access:

The beloved water licks me with its tongue,
soothing me all over.
The shadow of barbed wire,
like a tattoo on a slave,
stretches sombre on my skin
and I wash and wash,
and fall into another reality.

In the title poem Zhiti is clinging to his humanity by the barest thread "I, gone mad, scream in silence: / Hi there, world! / You may have forgotten me, / but not I you." In a sense, because the regime fell in 1990; and Visar Zhiti finally got out of the gulag; this is a collection with a happy ending. The poet preserved his sanity, and prevailed. In 'The Tyrant's One-time Office Near Which I Work' he even gets to visit the office of his tormentor and - echoes of Hannah Arendt - finds it to be a duller place than he'd imagined: "No abyss of convictions. No gun barrels / Emerging from drawers / like the eyes of metal detectors. / I stood silent, pallid / As if just over a long illness."

This collection of poems was born out of one man's worst nightmare come true. It is one of those rare books with the power to fundamentally alter the way the reader thinks about the world. Buy it and keep it close. It is the starkest illustration I've seen yet of how the high Socialist hopes of the early twentieth century degenerated into such sordid everyday tyranny.

May, 2006

CAPITALIST ROADERS AND SCHOOLCHILDREN
MAO - The Unknown Story by Jung Chang and Jon Halliday, Random House 814 pages, $50 Canada ISBN 0-679-42271-4

That Mao was one of the most despicable individuals ever to exert significant influence in the world is now basically undeniable. The Chinese government may still publicly peddle the line that Mao was "seventy percent right, thirty percent wrong", but as present-day China continues its great free-market leap, the current crop of altogether more mild-mannered Beijing tyrants must know that Mao led their country on a egomaniacal adventure which almost destroyed it. Time was when Mao had his defenders in the West; those such as Jean Paul Sartre who in the 1960s praised Mao's use of violence as "profoundly moral". But the earnest faces of 1968 have now all melted into history. That was then. These days, instead of falling at the feet of tyrants, the Western Left, for the most part, prefers to believe in nothing at all.

The most obvious question hovering over this biography is 'what does it tell us, that we didn't already know?' So much has already been written about Mao; long before this book appeared we knew that he was a very bad man indeed. The answer mostly lies in the amount of new forensic detail Chang and Halliday provide: they put flesh on the bones of the Mao story, from the Communist Seizure of power in 1949 to China's opportunistic rapprochement with United States in 1972. But they also tell us much Mao's early involvement in politics. In 1911, when Mao was seventeen years old, the Republican Revolution brought an end to over two thousand years of imperial rule. In the spring of 1913, the nineteen year old Mao entered teacher training college. In the open-minded atmosphere in the aftermath of the fall of the Manchu monarchy, Chinese youth experienced real political freedom:

"The students were exposed to all sorts of new ideas and encouraged to think freely and organise study groups. They turned out publications about anarchism, nationalism and Marxism, and for a while a portrait of Marx hung in the auditorium."

Far from being any sort of oppressed proletarian, Mao was a typical student radical.

"Mao had earlier come across the word "socialism" in a newspaper. Now he encountered "communism" for the first time... Mao was not a loner, and, like students the world over, he and his friends talked long and hard... On summer evenings they climbed the hill behind the school and sat arguing deep into the night on the grass where crickets crooned and glow-worms twinkled, ignoring the summons of the bugle to bed."

One gets the impression that, had things been different, after his initial dabbling with radical politics, Mao might have settled down to become just another jaded professorial type who once believed in the Revolution but discovered it had no practical application in the real world, and so got a job teaching in a Sociology Department near you.

The book does have its flaws: Chang and Halliday tend to portray the young Mao as if he never really believed in anything and his whole involvement in the Communist movement was just a play for personal power. This isn't credible. It is one thing to join a movement on the verge of, or already in, power for Machiavellian reasons. But who in their right mind - and whatever else Mao was, he was no fool - would join a fringe political group, which the Chinese Communist Party (CCP) was when Mao joined it in 1921, purely for personal advancement? To characterise Mao's decision to join the CCP - twenty eight years before it came to power - as being just another example of his undoubted later opportunism is stretching credibility. No doubt the young Mao was an arrogant little swine, as many student activists are. But political belief must have played some role in his early life. He couldn't have known then, that things would go so dramatically in his favour; and that he would grow up to become the all-powerful Chairman Mao.

I have long thought that inside many student leftists lurks a little Mao Tse-tung. For better or for worse, most of them grow up to be accountants or software engineers. By dealing with Mao as a three dimensional human personality, we can apply the lessons of his hideous legacy to the everyday. By turning him into a purely evil monster, something inhuman, as Chang and Halliday occasionally do, we make him nothing to do with us. One of the crucial lessons of twentieth century history is precisely that the Stalins, the Hitlers, the Maos, the Pol Pots are everything to do with us.

That said, the chapters on the Cultural Revolution (1966-72) are a brilliant exposé of what was perhaps the most cynical political manoeuvre in all human history. Like most decisions in his mature political career, its aim was to strengthen Mao's grip on power. Mao used his wife, the former actress Jiang Qing, to whip school students up into a frenzy, turning them first on teachers, academics and artists and then on Mao's opponents in the state apparatus. The Cultural Revolution was made possible because of a deal Mao made with former Defence Minister Lin Biao: a powerful figure in the regime and someone to whom Mao often turned when a dirty job needed doing. The upshot was that army Chief of Staff, Lou Ruiqing, a long time ally of Mao's but someone against whom Lin Biao bore a long-standing grudge, would face the entirely fabricated charge of high treason; in return Lin would enthusiastically endorse Madame Mao's 'Kill Culture' manifesto.

After the failure of the Great Leap Forward, which instead of the promised prosperity had led to famine, Mao's position was weak. His opponents within the Communist Party were real as well as imaginary.

Only when Lin's support was secured did Mao feel confident enough to let Jiang Qing off her leash. On August 18th Mao stood next to Lin Biao on Tiananmen Gate while Lin told the self-styled student 'Red Guards' to go throughout the country and "smash old culture".

But Mao wanted something much more vicious. On 23 August he told the new authorities that "…Peking is too civilised… That afternoon groups of teenage Red Guards descended on the courtyard of the Peking Writers Association… Red Guards rained blows with their heavy belts on some two dozen of the country's best known writers. Large insulting wooden plaques were hung on thin wire from the writers' necks, as they were thrashed in the scorching sun. One of the victims was the sixty-nine year old writer Lao She, who had been lauded by the regime as "the people's artist". The following day, he drowned himself in a lake."

It is bad enough that during this period, deluded young people in the Western world began carrying pictures of Chairman Mao on political demonstrations; but someone like Jean Paul Sartre should have known better. Under General De Gaulle, who was President of France at this time, French writers such as Sartre enjoyed freedoms their Chinese contemporaries couldn't even have dreamt of, because they were too busy begging their torturers to stop.

The next targets were "capitalist roaders" within the regime itself. As ever, the charges against those jailed, tortured and executed were usually part paranoid fantasy, part barefaced lie. It was the Chinese version of Stalin's 1930s show-trials. The methods were very different:

"Stalin had carried out his purges using an elite, the KGB who swiftly hustled their victims out of sight to prison, gulag or death. Mao made sure that such violence and humiliation was carried out in public, and he vastly increased the number of persecutors by getting his victims tormented and tortured by their own direct subordinates."

But the result was similar: all dissent (actual and imagined) was throttled by the rampaging schoolchildren; and Mao's power became absolute. Mao's particular genius was that he co-opted potential discontent among the youth, and used it for his own savage ends. During this period China broke decisively with the Soviet Union and pursued an aggressively independent foreign policy; even cultivating its own satellite states. The two most notable of these were Enver Hoxha's Albania and Pol Pot's Democratic Republic of Kampuchea; regimes whose unadulterated madness made even Mao seem mild in comparison.

The ironic twist is that all this led China not towards some 'purer' version of socialism, but towards an alliance of convenience with the USA from 1972 onwards, and its current free-market leap forward. The computer I am writing this review on bears the inscription: made in China. However, Internet users in China probably won't be able to read this review, when it goes online. In many ways the story of Mao's tyrannical regime hasn't ended, but goes on. It is a ghastly Machiavellian tale which this beautifully written biography throws some sharp new light on.

Summer, 2006

A CRITIQUE OF *RED LAMP*: THE JOURNAL OF REALIST, SOCIALIST AND HUMANITARIAN POETRY

It has often been said, that if only we (poets) spent less time pursuing the seemingly endless aesthetics versus politics argument, and more time actually writing poetry, then the world (or at least the part of it which appreciates poetry) would probably be a better place. After all, aren't we free to write whatever poetry we so choose? And it is certainly now possible (at least in the US and Britain) to find publishing outlets for almost any variety of poetry. Why don't you just get on with it?! So goes the frustrated cry of those who probably suspect that, deep down, we're the sort of people who like nothing better than to drone on all night about 'form versus content' until even the cat is desperately beseeching us, to please let her out in the rain! At least out there she won't have to listen to us whinging on about L=A=N=G=U=A=G=E Poetry or Socialist Realism.

And I have to say that, despite the fact I really do think that there are important issues involved here; such as, for example, which poetic talents get nurtured, encouraged and promoted, and which suffer from neglect or are ignored; there have also been times when, like my metaphorical cat, I would have given anything to escape the sort of infantile carry on - the literary equivalent of a bad third division football match - which all too often passes for criticism/debate, between those who champion language for its own sake, and those who champion social/political content.

On one side we have the poetry 'aesthete', the guy who hangs around the poetry cafe all day long, a volume of L=A=N=G=U=A=G=E poetry in one hand, his Portable Nietzsche in the other, doing his bit for the avant-garde, with a little help from a tea-cosy hat, probably knitted for him by his mother. Ask him what sort of poetry he likes and he'll tell you that, in his opinion, Clark Coolidge (who?!) is his generation's answer to Gertrude Stein. Hand him a copy of a meaningless poem in which 'Saddam Hussein's pyjamas' rhymes with 'llamas' and he will, I guarantee you, be very impressed. Tell him you wrote it and he'll probably tell you that, in his opinion, you're the next big thing, perhaps even, if you're lucky, your generation's answer to Clark Coolidge.

Meanwhile, on the other side of the table, sits the poetry-bolshevik, the peak of his Russian cap at all times turned up to signify his utter contempt for all bourgeois authority. Look closely and you'll see, pinned to this self-same cap, a small red star. Ask him where he got it and he'll proudly tell you that it originally belonged to his late uncle Stan, who was a member of the Communist Party and the Electrical Trades Union during the 1950s. Ask him what sort of poetry he likes and he'll probably mention Pablo Neruda, Vladimir Mayakovsky, Langston Hughes... Nothing wrong with that, you may say.

But then show him a copy of a 'poem' you 'wrote' about fifteen years ago. Make it an angry/earnest broadside about the decline of an inner city area of, say, Liverpool or Glasgow under the Tories, and bring it to the following rapturous conclusion: "Thatcher is a cow. / Get her out now!" As he reads it, jabber on about how you submitted it to *The Times Literary Supplement, The London Review of Books, The New Yorker* etc. but that they all rejected it, preferring instead to publish the usual rubbish from the likes of Ashbery, Updike and Brodsky. As he hands you back your masterpiece, the poetry-bolshevik will earnestly inform you that a bourgeois publication such as *The Times Literary Supplement* would never dream of publishing a political poem such as this. You'll smile wryly, say that you were naive to send it to them in the first place, and then he'll suggest that you should, perhaps, consider sending it to a magazine called *Red Lamp*. He has the address here somewhere...

Now, of course, I'm not suggesting that we should at all times be brutally honest, when it comes to other people's poetry. There are things like feelings to consider. And sometimes poets, particularly those from non-academic backgrounds, start off writing the sort of substandard political doggerel parodied above, but do, in time, improve to such an extent that they end up writing poems which have real artistic merit. So, we shouldn't come down on fledgling poets like a ton of bricks, while they're still trying to find their feet as best they can. But neither should we give false encouragement by helping substandard verse prematurely into print. The truth is that, in the long run, and sometimes even in the short run, this sort of help is no help at all, because once a mediocre poem is out in the public domain, even in a small magazine with a relatively modest print-run, then it is fair game for hostile critics. And, as you well know, there is absolutely no shortage of them.

A magazine such as *Red Lamp* could become an important meeting place for poets who are outside the political mainstream, a place where the issues, which we constantly come up against, such as, for example, the disastrous legacy of Stalinist Socialist Realism, could be properly dealt with. It could also provide a forum for the development of a thoughtful critique of the rest of the poetry world. Why not review the latest collections by big name poets such as, say, Simon Armitage, Carol Ann Duffy or Paul Durcan? Surely we must have something to say about all of them. There is so much more that we could be doing.

But as things stand, *Red Lamp* is, I think, in some danger of becoming a magazine content to preach to a dwindling band of converts. The fact is that, world-wide, there probably aren't enough talented politically conscious poets to fill your pages with quality work issue after issue. (And quality is definitely what we should all be aiming at.)

So, in one sense, it's hardly surprising, that there are several poems in issue 9, which fall far short of what's required. Meryl Brown Tobin's *Poem of Witness* is one example:

After days of massacre,
Indonesia allows
U.N. in.
Australia leads.
'Vested interests
in oil,' cry protestors.
Multi-millionaire chides:
'Australia's going in solely
on humanitarian grounds -
She should think about
economic and trade concerns.'
What price humanity?

As poetry this sort of thing is an unmitigated disaster. The language is not in the slightest bit fresh or inventive. And the opinions expressed are nothing that a Blair/Clinton pseudo-liberal couldn't at least pretend to agree with. Even in terms of content, it falls absolutely flat. And Steven Katsineris's *For Unity and Equality* is no better. It starts off weakly enough:

If you're Anglo-Australian then you don't know how it feels
to be born ethnic in Australia.
To be verbally abused or worse,
made to feel you're off the last boat...

But it was the last few lines that really made me cringe:

If you're Anglo-Australian you can't really know how it feels,
that's not your fault, but you can try to listen, learn and understand.
And let Aboriginal and Ethnic Australians know
they don't stand alone, that many Anglo-Australians
stand alongside them too, standing up for unity and equality.

Well-meaning it may be, but good poetry it most definitely is not. Reading a poem like this is, for me, about as aesthetically pleasing as bathing in cold porridge. It is offensive on two levels. Firstly as someone who has, on occasion, spent days (if not weeks) struggling to find exactly the right words to make a poem as complete as I possibly can, I find the bland, lazy language astonishing. And secondly, I know perfectly well that this is exactly the sort of poem which hostile reviewers will use to beat everyone who contributes to *Red Lamp* over the head with. "This is what happens", they will tell us, "when you try to mix poetry and politics..."

And we can hardly blame them. If you offer the opposing team an open goal, then you forfeit the right to complain, when they stick the ball in the back of the net.

There were, of course, also a number of good poems in issue 9, such as Julie Ashpool's *Sister* and Vincent Berquez's *Hunter of Work?*, for example. And I particularly liked Susan Stanford's *Poor Man*:

Dismissed, shrinking into himself, he inhales
the poisons of two packs a day. What's the point
now? He's out of the picture. Vision's become
another management buzzword. Life's gritty,
takes longer. He walks or travels by bus,
does his washing by hand. Food's just short enough
for thought to be called for. He mashes sardines.
Puts a match to the gas. Feels the cold at the tip
of his nose. A moment of toast in the mouth.

But as *Red Lamp* goes on, poems of the inferior variety increasingly seem to predominate. And it was that fact which spurred me to write this piece. The criticisms I make are made only in the hope of stirring up a constructive debate from which a stronger magazine might perhaps emerge...

August, 2001

PROTEST IN GENOA, AN IRISHWOMAN'S DIARY
by Maureen Gallagher (43pp 3.OO Euros)

As its title suggests this beautifully produced booklet, in which poet Maureen Gallagher tells from the inside the story of the huge anti-capitalist protest at the 2001 G8 summit, has ambitions to be both a personal memoir and a politically motivated pamphlet of the old variety. Its forty three glossy pages contain no less than twenty six photographs of the dramatic events in Genoa, during which one protester, Carlo Giuliani, was shot dead by Italian police.

The fact that Gallagher is an accomplished poet of whom, I have no doubt, much more will be heard, gave me hope that this would amount to more than another political broadcast on behalf of the righteous and the dour. The result? Well, it's mixed. Gallagher is good at building drama, and succeeds admirably in giving the reader a sense of what it must have been like to face the tear gas and the riot police. In her description of the demonstration she shows us that, despite all the earnest faces, the anti-capitalist movement has a sense of humour too:

"As we proceeded along the streets, women waved knickers and underpants from windows in defiance of Berlusconi's order that there was to be no underwear visible on clotheslines hanging from high rise flats."

Apparently, the Italian Prime Minister thought visiting dignitaries might be offended by the sight of Italian women's underwear.

Elsewhere, though, *Protest In Genoa* falters rather: activists have conversations which are so banal that all one can do is hope they never actually happened:

"Keith told me that Jeffrey Archer… had just been sentenced to four years for corruption and contempt of court. 'It would be great to see some of our lot doing time for corruption', I remarked. Unfortunately, there wouldn't be enough room in your prisons for them!' Keith quipped."

And on page nine we are told:

"As it turned out, on Saturday night no one was in the least interested in Bob Dylan [who was in concert at a venue ten miles away] or his jaded performance: there were much more serious and real issues to be attended to."

For me this simply didn't ring true. No large group of people is ever that uniformly earnest: every demo has the guy who only came along in the hope that he might get laid. And, in my experience, he at least is always interested in talking about Bob Dylan.

February, 2004

THE STORY OF O
by Olaf Tyaransen

Olaf Tyaransen's autobiography is unusual in that it is difficult to know where it belongs in the broader scheme of things. The fact that the author is only 29 years old tends to make one a little suspicious. Is this simply a super-cool *Hot Press* version of the sort of pretty-boy autobiography we have come to expect from the likes of Ronan Keating and David Beckam? Or does Tyaransen's 215 page account of his own short life actually tell us anything worth knowing, either about the man himself or the circles he moves in?

The account of his escapades in Galway makes for interesting reading. Having grown up in Galway myself, it was amusing to see mention of places such as Brambles Cafe and The Savoy Arcade; venues, which, in the 1980s, were the centre of the world for teenagers here. Tyaransen grew up in the suburb of Barna and attended St. Enda's College, where he once asked Bishop Eamonn Casey "where in the Ten Commandments did it tell us that 'Thou shalt not wear a condom?' " Tyaransen says that, by the time he crossed swords with our beloved former Bishop, he had "already gotten [his] sex education from Judy Blume and Anais Nin."

Also of interest is his early involvement in the local music and arts scene. In the early 90s Tyaransen worked for a free sheet called *The Word*, began to write poetry, went to The Warwick nightclub a lot and got drunk, stoned and laid with a regularity normally reserved for rock-stars. He looks back on those days as a kind of lost Golden Age: "At the beginning of the 1990s, for a couple of halcyon years, Galway was undoubtedly the best city in Ireland (nay Europe) for any aspiring musician, writer, actor or artist to land in; almost overnight becoming a magnet for myriad minstrels of all nationalities and artistic persuasions." Of course, we've heard variations on this theme a thousand times before. However, Tyaransen does capture something of Galway during this period, when the recession-ridden 80s where finally over, but the atmosphere was still relatively relaxed.

As well as being a rock journalist Tyaransen is, of course, a published poet. *The Consequences of Slaughtering Butterflies* was published by Salmon in 1992. He is also one of those people for whom simply taking drugs is never enough. He has to constantly tell us about it as well. In chapter ten he outlines how cocaine helped him get published: "Say what you want about cocaine but there's no denying it stimulates the mind. I wrote six complete poems that morning, and made rough notes for as many more, all in the space of about two and a half feverishly intoxicated hours... They just kept coming." He then sent these to Jessie Lendennie with a "brief covering letter." It's difficult to know how seriously we are meant to take all this. Is Tyaransen playing to the 'rock and roll!' gallery? Or is he really asking us to take this sort of thing at face value? Either way, one suspects that the reality was probably somewhat more mundane.

During the account of his *Hot Press* years *The Story Of O* moves on from being just occasionally annoying and becomes increasingly insufferable. On the one hand, Tyaransen's sole mission in life seems to be to meet as many famous people as possible. The book includes photographs of Tyaransen meeting Bono, Allen Ginsberg, P.J. O'Rourke, Irvine Welsh and former super-model Christy Turlington. But, on the other hand, he sometimes takes himself far too seriously altogether. The worst example of this is when he recalls his campaign as a Legalise Cannabis candidate in the 1997 General Election. Tyaransen accuses fellow pro-Cannabis candidate, Ming The Merciless [Luke Flanagan] of "playing into the hands of the prohibitionists" and pompously declares, in a line which could have been borrowed from Bono: "If you want to subvert something, you need to do it from within." It should be remembered that Ming, as well as making us laugh, actually received more votes in Galway West than Tyaransen did in Dun Laoghaire.

The Story Of O could, perhaps, have been rescued by a strong injection of self-depreciating humour, but Tyaransen is not at all anxious to laugh at himself. Maybe he's worried that, if he started laughing, he might not be able to stop.

Spring, 2001

WHY CHÈ GUEVARA MATTERS

Chè Guevara And The Cuban Revolution by Mike Gonzalez (Bookmarks, £8 Stg 186 pp,)

Since the statues of Lenin were toppled and the USSR was suddenly no more, the old Marxist left has suffered an extraordinary existential crisis. Some of the comrades have swapped their old belief in all things working-class for an aggressive conservatism typically found on the dark side of *The Sunday Independent.*

Despite this ideological collapse, the image of Chè Guevara has survived to adorn a million earnest T-shirts; as he has become one of the icons of the new, and much less rigidly ideological, anti-capitalist movement: "There is now an entirely new generation who instantly recognise the deep eyes and beard of Guevara, who wear the T-shirt and buy the enormous variety of consumer goods that carry that famous image."

Mike Gonzalez examines the roots of Guevara's contemporary appeal, and looks at his life and politics in some detail. Despite Guevara's belief that the rural poor of countries like Cuba, Bolivia, and the Congo were the battering-ram with which capitalism would ultimately be broken, and a new socialist era ushered in; he himself was in many ways the quintessential middle-class radical, his family coming "from a cattle-raising oligarchy with distant links to Ireland on the one side and the Spanish colonial elite on the other".

Unlike many middle-class radicals Guevara had the willpower and courage to see his struggle through to its bitter end in a remote and mountainous region of rural Bolivia, where on October 9 1967 he was killed "in the village schoolroom of La Higuera by the Bolivian army under the watchful eye of US military advisors".

Gonzalez is informative on how the Cuban revolutionaries were forced by US hostility and economic sanctions into the close relationship they came to have with the USSR. He also puts to bed the notion that US hostility to Castro's Cuba is some sort of protest against the lack of democracy there; before the revolution of New Year's Eve 1958 Cuba was ruled by the Mafia-friendly dictator Batista and the State Department had no complaints.

Given he has to deal with such a vast range of material, from the politics of Guevara's native Argentina to his later guerilla adventures in the Congo, it's hardly surprising that Gonzalez sometimes tends to skim the surface of important events where he could have dug a little deeper.

That said, Gonzalez's brisk and populist style mostly serves his subject well. The weaker passages are those towards the end where he lapses into fairly crude propagandistic mode; the strongest those in which he lets Guevara's revolutionary personality shine through to show the reader how politics can sometimes be about so much more than spin and smiles for the camera.

October, 2004

UTOPIANS VERSUS REALISTS?
Citizenship and Racism: The case against McDowell's Referendum by Kieran Allen
(38pps) published by Bookmarks Ireland.

This pamphlet makes the case against the proposed change to our Constitution which if passed, will result in children born on the island of Ireland losing the automatic right to citizenship.

Kieran Allen points out that, if the referendum succeeds, someone born in Boston to parents who have lived all their lives in America would be entitled to come here, claim Social Welfare and play for the Irish soccer team, as long as they have one Irish grandparent; while a child born to a Filipino nurse working in a Dublin hospital (and paying taxes to the Irish Government) could be denied.

Far from being about clearing up an anomaly, Allen argues, this referendum is an attempt to put 'another brick in the wall' of a system of institutionalised racism.

Citizenship and Racism is strong on facts and figures, and deals in detail with myths about asylum-seekers supposedly getting preferential treatment in housing and social welfare. It also makes much of the way wealthy tax-exiles, such as JP MacManus and Dermot Desmond, are able to avail of most of the benefits of Irish citizenship, while avoiding the lifelong relationship the rest of us inevitably come to have with the Revenue Commissioners.

One of Allen's arguments is that despite the Government's presentation of its policy as the only common-sense approach; the attempt to control immigration is an utterly utopian ideal: "We live in a world where capital scours the globe in search of profit... In such a global economy, immigration is a fact of life. Pretending to outlaw it... limiting the numbers is like pretending there won't be sex before marriage - or that it will happen in small doses and be strictly controlled."

Such pragmatic considerations aside, there is something morally reprehensible about an ideology which allows money such freedom, but attempts to use the arbitrary borders of the European Union to control the movement of human beings.

That said, when he tries to offer an alternative vision, Allen falters: "We can live in a society where there is an exciting flowering of different dresses, foods... abolish passports... border checkpoints... by uprooting the system of capitalism which has created all these relics."

The difficulty with this is it ignores the extent to which the 'socialist alternative' Allen advocates has been discredited by what became of the Soviet Union, and people's experience here of an often inefficient, unaccountable public sector.

If your average Josephine thinks socialism means turning the world into one giant FAS scheme, then she'll always go back to listening to Michael McDowell. This is a question Kieran Allen and others on the far Left must face; but one this pamphlet ultimately leaves unanswered.

SYNGE'S INNOCENT CONCERN FOR RURAL IRELAND

Travels In Wicklow, West Kerry And Connemara (Serif Travel) was originally published in 1911, two years after John Millington Synge's death, with drawings by Jack B Yeats, which are reproduced here.

Travels In Wicklow... is in many ways a typical product of the Celtic Twilight: a travelogue in which Synge - arguably our greatest, certainly our most influential, playwright - turns his face starkly away from the class-ridden city of Dublin in the lead-up to the 1913 Lockout, to seek out the 'real' Ireland in places like Wicklow, Dingle, Bellmullet and Carraroe.

In the section 'The vagrants of Wicklow' Synge says: "In this life, however, there are many privileges. The tramp in Ireland is little troubled by the laws, and lives in out-of-door conditions that keep him in good humour and fine bodily health." It is believable that rural Ireland 100 years ago was more tolerant of those who had fallen out of society, than we are now. In those days a vagrant on the road between Arklow and Bray would have faced less interference from the forces of law and respectability than someone living a similar lifestyle in Galway city today. But it is unlikely that sleeping out in the open - before global warming brought us the golden Octobers we currently enjoy - would have kept the vagrants of the day in anything approaching "fine bodily health".

However, Synge was disturbed by the poverty in Connemara, which was on a different scale to anything he'd have seen in Wicklow. "It is part of the misfortune of Ireland that nearly all the characteristics which give colour and attractiveness to Irish life are bound up with a social condition that is near to penury, while in countries like Brittany the best external features of the local life - the rich embroidered dresses ... the carved furniture - are connected with a decent and comfortable social condition," he wrote.

He wasn't all earnest social comment, though. The section on Spiddal proves Synge was also a keen observer of women, or girls, as he liked to call them: "In a district like Spiddal one sees curious gradations of types, especially on Sunday and holidays... a few of them, especially the girls, magnificently built!"

In the closing chapter Synge offers "possible remedies" to the conditions he encountered In "the worst districts of Mayo and Connemara". His conclusion was that Ireland needed something more than piecemeal economic and agricultural reform: "If Home Rule would not of itself make a national life ... it would do more than half a million creameries." Synge may not have been any sort of revolutionary, but neither was he the sort of liberal pedant who thinks the problems of the world can always be sorted out by a bit of fine-tuning here and there.

From this juncture Synge seems to have been something of a concerned innocent. This innocence would, surely, have been much diminished had he lived to see the Ireland he knew vanish into the breach opened by the Great War and the 1916 Rising. It is interesting to speculate how he might then have developed as a literary artist. Yeats' poetry was transformed by these events; no doubt Synge's plays would have been too.

November, 2005